LINGUISTICS
PSYCHOLINGUISTICS
AND THE TEACHING
OF READING

An Annotated Bibliography
Compiled by Kenneth S. Goodman
and
Yetta M. Goodman
University of Arizona

Third Edition, 1980

Published by the
INTERNATIONAL READING ASSOCIATION
800 Barksdale Road • Newark, Delaware 19711

INTERNATIONAL READING ASSOCIATION

**OFFICERS
1980-1981**

President   Olive S. Niles, State Department of Education, Hartford, Connecticut

Vice President   Kenneth S. Goodman, University of Arizona, Tucson, Arizona

Vice President-Elect   Jack Cassidy, Millersville State College, Millersville, Pennsylvania

Executive Director   Ralph C. Staiger, International Reading Association, Newark, Delaware

DIRECTORS

Term Expiring Spring 1981
  Norma Dick, Clovis Unified School District, Clovis, California
  Eleanor M. Ladd, University of South Carolina, Spartanburg, South Carolina
  John C. Manning, University of Minnesota, Minneapolis, Minnesota

Term Expiring Spring 1982
  Nicholas P. Criscuolo, New Haven Public Schools, New Haven, Connecticut
  Bernice E. Cullinan, New York University, New York, New York
  Patricia S. Koppman, San Diego Unified Schools, San Diego, California

Term Expiring Spring 1983
  Elizabeth Hunter-Grundin, Schools Council, London, England
  Alden J. Moe, Purdue University, West Lafayette, Indiana
  Dianne L. Monson, University of Washington, Seattle, Washington

Copyright 1980 by the
International Reading Association, Inc.
Library of Congress Cataloging in Publication Data
Goodman, Kenneth S.
  Linguistics, psycholinguistics, and the
  teaching of reading.
  Authors' names in reverse order in other editions.
  1. Reading—Bibliography. I. Goodman, Yetta M., 1931-   joint author. II. Title.
  Z5818.L3G66   1980   [LB1050]   016.4284'07   80-16364
  ISBN 0-87207-312-2

CONTENTS

    Introduction   v

1   Beginning Reading

6   Comprehension, Semantics, and Meaning

18   Curriculum

20   Language Differences: Dialects, Bilingualism, Biliteracy, and Sociolinguistics

26   Discourse Analysis

31   General Applications of Linguistics and Psycholinguistics to Reading

37   Instruction in Reading

45   Miscue Analysis

49   Relationship between Oral and Written Language

57   The Reading Teacher and Linguistics

61   Syntax, Grammar, and Intonation

66   Testing and Evaluation

68   Theories of Reading

74   Words

IRA PUBLICATIONS COMMITTEE 1980-1981   Robert B. Ruddell, University of California at Berkeley, *Chairing* • Phylliss Adams, University of Denver • Alison Bellack, Largo (Florida) C & I Center • Janet R. Binkley, IRA • Faye R. Branca, IRA • Jerry L. Johns, Northern Illinois University • Lloyd W. Kline, IRA • Carol Kuykendall, Houston (Texas) Public Schools • Eleanor M. Ladd, University of South Carolina at Spartanburg • Grover Matthewson, Florida International University • Christina Neal, St. Albans, West Virginia • Joan Nelson, State University of New York at Binghamton • Lloyd O. Ollila, University of Victoria • P. David Pearson, University of Illinois at Champaign • María Elena Rodriguez, Asociacion Internacional de Lectura, Buenos Aires • Carol Sager, Chestnut Hill, Massachusetts • S. Jay Samuels, University of Minnesota • Lyndon W. Searfoss, Arizona State University • Ralph C. Staiger, IRA • Judith Thelen, Frostburg (Maryland) State College • Joanna Williams, Teachers College, Columbia University.

The International Reading Association attempts, through its publications, to provide a forum for a wide spectrum of opinion on reading. This policy permits divergent viewpoints without assuming the endorsement of the Association.

INTRODUCTION

This annotated bibliography covers the professional literature relating to linguistics, psycholinguistics, and reading. In 1967 when we first attempted that task, we could feel confident that we had fully covered the topic. Almost nothing had appeared before 1960. The second edition appeared in 1971. Considerably more pertinent literature had appeared in the interim than in all the previous years. The entries increased by 40 percent with much more stringent screening. Topics had expanded and diversified and alternate positions had emerged. Still, we could feel that we could truly be inclusive in our attempt "to provide as extensive a bibliography as possible without undue redundancy."

Our task for this third edition has been much more difficult. Applications of linguistics and psycholinguistics to reading have become pervasive and foundational to the work in many aspects of reading. New concerns, such as discourse analysis, have emerged. The interdisciplinary and cross-disciplinary nature of applications to reading have caused the base of publications to spill over into linguistic and psychological literature. More literature had to be read in a wider range of sources and much had to be screened out.

We used these criteria for our screening:
The relationship of linguistics and psycholinguistics to the content of the selection must be more than incidental.
The selection must represent a sound application of some school of linguistics or psycholinguistics.
The selection must not be simply a summary of the work of others or a restatement of another work by the same author.
The selection must not be so dated that it is superceded by more definitive work by the author or other scholars.
The content must deal with an aspect of significance to reading process, learning, or instruction.

Perhaps our most difficult decisions were related to how far we should extend the scope of this bibliography. We could have included general language arts, ethnography, and language development—all with some justification. To keep our task within useful bounds, we had to exclude these topics and others.

In the second edition, we isolated research in a separate heading to highlight the emergence of such linguistically sophisticated research. But such research has exploded and come to virtually dominate the literature so we have included here research studies under the topical headings with other publications.

In the 1971 edition, we had a section on intonation. There has been little written in that area in recent years, so we've combined it with the section on syntax, since intonation in oral reading tends to reflect and indicate syntactic patterns. We've separated out selections dealing with beginning reading, testing, and miscue analysis to offer better focus. We've also added a section on discourse analysis—an area of intense activity in recent years. It culminates a continuous trend toward interest in larger language units and away from an earlier preoccupation with letter-sound relationships. The major focus now in psycholinguistic application in reading is the nature and comprehension of whole texts; it is on the role of writer and reader in communication through written language.

We do not mean to imply by our categorization of the field that our headings are the only ones possible and that they do not overlap. Rather, we have used divisions which we feel represent major areas of activity and useful ways of classifying the literature.

A number of people have played roles in developing this third edition. Among them are Bette-Jean Kasurak, John Pollack, Myna Haussler, and Claudia Dybdahl. We thank them and all the others who helped.

KSG
YMG

BEGINNING READING

In recent years, there has been increased interest in theory and research on the beginnings of literacy as language development. Much of this work parallels what has been happening in the study of oral language development and moves beyond a preoccupation (in earlier publications) with beginning instruction.

ADAMS, MARILYN JAGER, RICHARD C. ANDERSON, and DOLORES DURKIN. "Beginning Reading: Theory and Practice," *Language Arts*, 55, 1 (January 1978), 19-25.

Discusses and responds to some of the problems encountered by beginning readers: word recognition, syntax and semantics, organization of text, and the relationship of oral and written language.

BEERS, JAMES W., and EDMUND H. HENDERSON. "A Study of Developing Orthographic Concepts among First Graders," *Research in the Teaching of English*, 11, 2 (Fall 1977), 133-148.

Explores first grade spelling errors and suggests a developmental pattern based first upon phonemic knowledge as characterized by articulatory features, and later reflecting lexical and syntactic information.

BLACHOWICZ, CAMILLE L.Z. "Metalinguistic Awareness and the Beginning Reader," *Reading Teacher*, 31, 8 (May 1978), 875-876.

Indicates that children must distinguish between units of language, such as words and sentences, before this terminology can be successfully used for instructional purposes.

CHOMSKY, CAROL. "Write Now, Read Later," *Childhood Education*, 47 (March 1971), 296-299.

Makes a case for children to learn to read by building on the base of their own invented spellings.

CHRISTIAN, CHESTER. "Preschool Literacy in Spanish," *Hispania*, 60, 3 (September 1977), 530-532.

Presents case studies of two year old readers. Emphasizes building on children's interests and iniative.

CLARK, MARGARET. *Young Fluent Readers*. London: Heinemann, 1976.

Studies preschool children who are reading prior to the primary school experience.

CLAY, MARIE M. "Reading Errors and Self-Correction Behavior," *British Journal of Educational Psychology*, 39 (February 1969), 47-56.

Describes the overt self-correction behavior of five year olds reading orally at regular intervals who were studied for a period of one year. Presents developmental results as well as results based on differences in reading ability. Data concerning substitution phenomena, syntactic constraints, and rates of self-correction are also given.

CLAY, MARIE M. *Reading: The Patterning of Complex Behaviour*. Auckland, New Zealand: Heinemann, 1972.

Presents information concerning beginning reading and the role of meaning. Describes a longitudinal study of children from five to eight years who come from differing language backgrounds in New Zealand.

CLAY, MARIE M. "A Syntactic Analysis of Reading Errors," *Journal of Verbal Learning and Verbal Behavior*, 7 (1968), 434-438.

Examines the oral reading of five year olds to see if their errors have structural equivalence to the correct response. Concludes that children's control over syntax dominates their reading behavior. Discovered that subjects corrected pronouns more than other parts of speech and single word substitutions more than sequence substitutions.

DOUGLASS, MALCOLM P. "Reading between and beyond the Lines," *Visible Language*, 7, 3 (Summer 1973), 225-234.

Views learning to read and write as similar to learning to speak and listen. Concludes that a natural development will occur if the child is given a supporting environment.

FORESTER, ANNE D. "Learning the Language of Reading: An Exploratory Study," *Alberta Journal of Educational Research*, 21 (1975), 56-62.

Stresses the parallel characteristics of learning to speak and learning to read through a study of the learning strategies and thought processes of the beginning teacher.

FOX, BARBARA CROWLEY. "How Children Analyze Language: Implications for Beginning Reading Instruction," *Reading Improvement*, 13, 4 (Winter 1976), 229-234.

Presents a review of research dealing with children's awareness of language and relating this to beginning reading instruction.

FRANCIS, HAZEL. "Children's Experience of Reading and Notions of Units in Language," *British Journal of Educational Psychology*, 43, 1 (February 1973), 17-23.

Investigates speech, reading, and writing in terms of children's concepts of instructional terminology and their identification of language units.

GOLDSTEIN, DAVID M. "Cognitive-Linguistic Functioning and Learning to Read in Preschoolers," *Journal of Educational Psychology*, 68, 6 (December 1976), 680-688.

Hypothesizes about interrelationships between cognitive-linguistic abilities of children aged five to seven and the process of beginning reading.

HOSKISSON, KENNETH. "Reading Readiness: Three Viewpoints," *Elementary School Journal*, 78, 1 (September 1977), 44-52.

Discusses reading readiness from the maturational, behaviorist, cognitive, and psycholinguistic viewpoints. Talks about the assisted reading strategy which is derived from psycholinguistic theory.

LADO, ROBERT. "Acquisition and Learning in Early Reading," *Hispania*, 60, 3 (September 1977), 533-535.

Discusses the relationship between language acquisition and learning in early reading. Claims that bilingual preschoolers learn to read more easily in Spanish than English.

MASON, JANA M. *Reading Readiness: A Definition and Skills Hierarchy from Preschoolers' Developing Concepts of Print*, Technical Report No. 59. Urbana-Champaign, Illinois: University of Illinois, Center for the Study of Reading, September 1977.

Identifies children's awareness of printed words and letters prior to the receiving of formal reading instruction. Concludes that children acquire their knowledge in the same order.

McDONELL, GLORIA M., and E. BESS OSBURN. "New Thoughts about Reading Readiness," *Language Arts*, 55, 1 (January 1978), 26-29.

Discusses reading readiness as an integration of visual and language conceptual systems.

NATCHEZ, G. "From Talking to Reading without Really Trying," *Reading Teacher*, 20 (January 1967), 339-421.

Suggests that universal acquisition of child language makes it possible for reading to be acquired through learning at one's own pace with continuous pride and excitement in accomplishment.

RESNICK, LOREN, and PHYLLIS WEAVER (Eds.). *Theory and Practice of Early Reading*, Volumes 1-3. Hillsdale, New Jersey: Erlbaum Associates, 1979.

Presents papers given at a conference on beginning reading. Includes the work of a number of psycholinguists considering aspects of language development, language function, the relationship of written language and not language in relationship to development of writing in young children.

RUDDELL, ROBERT B. "Reading Instruction in First Grade with Varying Emphasis on the Regularity of Grapheme-Phoneme Correspondences and the Relation of Language Structure to Meaning—Extended into Second Grade," *Reading Teacher*, 20 (May 1967), 730-739.

Compares children learning to read materials with varying degrees of grapheme-phoneme correspondences and materials with varying emphasis on language structure as related to meaning. Concludes that significant relationships exist between children's ability to control syntactic aspects of their oral language and their ability to comprehend written language.

RYSTROM, RICHARD. "Meaning and Structure," *Journal of Reading Behavior*, 5, 1 (Winter 1972-1973), 65-70.

Looks at beginning readers and the effects sentence structure has on the process of reading acquisition.

SMITH, FRANK. "Learning to Read by Reading," *Language Arts*, 53 (March 1976), 297-299.

Presents observations of the process of children trying to gain meaning from print.

SMITH, NILA BANTON. "Early Language Development: Foundation of Reading," *Elementary English*, 52, 3 (May 1975), 399-402, 418.

Presents research dealing with the theoretical notion that language development is an important contributor to reading.

SODERBERGH, RAGNILD. *Reading in Early Childhood*. Georgetown University Press, 1977.

Relates the experience of a linguist employing Doman's method to teach a child to read. Shows the modification of the method as a natural reading process begins to emerge in the child.

SPIEGEL, DIXIE LEE. "Meaning-Seeking Strategies for the Beginning Reader," *Reading Teacher*, 31, 7 (April 1978), 772-776.

Presents strategies to help the beginning reader gain meaning from text. Includes discussions of risk taking, self-monitoring, and self-correction.

TEALE, WILLIAM H. "Positive Environments for Learning to Read: What Studies of Early Readers Tell Us," *Language Arts*, 55, 8 (November-December 1978), 922-932.

Describes a literate environment for beginning readers based on research from the fields of psycholinguistics and early reading.

WARDHAUGH, RONALD. "Theories of Language Acquisition in Relation to Beginning Reading Instruction," *Reading Research Quarterly*, 7 (1971), 168-194.

Discusses various theories of language acquisition and finds them lacking when applied to current controversial topics. Also examines the differences between learning language and learning to read and concludes that application of language acquisition theories to beginning reading instruction is not worthwhile.

YLISTO, INGRID P. "Early Reading Responses of Young Finnish Children," *Reading Teacher*, 31, 2 (November 1977), 167-172.

Traces the development of reading behaviors in Finnish children when beginning instruction concentrates on phoneme-grapheme relationships. Results indicate that children have developed contextual and semantic strategies for word recognition prior to receiving instruction.

COMPREHENSION, SEMANTICS, AND MEANING

These selections deal with comprehension and semantic pragmatic aspects of language. In the general introduction, we commented on the shift in the field to concern with whole texts and readers' comprehension of them and away from small language units and patterns of letter-sound relationships. Although many of the discourse analysis selections relate strongly to comprehension, we've listed those selections separately so that users of this bibliography could get a sense of developments in discourse analysis as a subfield of psycholinguistic applications in reading.

AQUINO, MILAGROS, LUDWIG MOSBERG, and MARGE SHARRON. "Reading Comprehension Difficulty as a Function of Content Area and Linguistic Complexity," *Journal of Experimental Education*, 32 (Summer 1969), 1-4.

Explores the relationship between newspaper articles in different content areas of science, television, and human interest with differences of linguistic complexity which might affect comprehension as tested by cloze test procedures. These were related to reading ability test scores.

ARTLEY, A. STERL. "Words, Words, Words," *Language Arts*, 52, 8 (November-December 1975), 1067-1072.

Investigates comprehension as being an interaction between deep structures and surface structures of the language.

ASHER, STEVEN R. *Influence of Topic Interest on Black Children's and White Children's Reading Comprehension*, Technical Report No. 99. Urbana-Champaign, Illinois: University of Illinois, Center for the Study of Reading, July 1978.

Experiments with reducing the gap in reading achievement between black and white students by using high interest reading material. Finds that both groups of students have similar interests and both increase proportionally in scores.

ASHER, STEVEN R., SHELLEY HYMEL, and ALLAN WIGFIELD. *Children's Comprehension of High and Low Interest Materials and a Comparison of Two Cloze Scoring Methods*, Technical Report No. 17. Urbana-Champaign, Illinois: University of Illinois, Center for the Study of Reading, November 1976.

Provides experimental support for the theory that children comprehend high interest material better than low interest material.

ASKOV, EUNICE N., JANE LUBAUS, and KARLYN KAMM. "Syntactical Inferences with Reading Comprehension: A Beginning Step in Research," *Journal of Educational Research*, 71, 2 (November-December 1977), 76-80.

Examines one syntactic structure—that of embedding between subject and verb. Tries to identify its effects on young readers' comprehension.

BICKLEY, A.C., BILLIE J. ELLINGTON, and RACHEL T. BICKLEY. "The Cloze Procedure: A Conspectus," *Journal of Reading Behavior*, 2 (Summer 1970), 232-249.

Presents a comprehensive review of research in the cloze procedure in relation to readability, comprehension, language, and methodology.

BLACHOWICZ, CAMILLE L.Z. "Semantic Constructivity in Children's Comprehension," *Reading Research Quarterly*, 13, 2 (1977-1978), 188-199.

Experiments with the ability of children and adults to recognize semantically congruent items after reading short paragraphs. Finds that congruent influences are identified as having been in the original reading selection.

BORMUTH, JOHN R. "The Cloze Readability Procedure," *Elementary English*, 45 (April 1968), 429-436.

Outlines cloze readability procedures for classroom use to determine difficulty of instructional materials. Presents a case for the validity of cloze procedures.

BORMUTH, JOHN R. "An Operational Definition of Comprehension Instruction," in Kenneth S. Goodman and James T. Fleming (Eds.), *Psycholinguistics and the Teaching of Reading*. Newark, Delaware: International Reading Association, 1969, 48-60.

Rejects much of the research on reading comprehension because it has been based on too vague a notion of what comprehension is. Advances a new definition: the ability "to acquire and exhibit information gained as a consequence of reading printed language."

BORMUTH, JOHN R., and others. "Children's Comprehension of between and within Sentence Syntactic Structures," *Journal of Educational Psychology*, 61 (May 1970), 349-357.

Investigates three classes of syntactic forms (intrasentence, intersentence, and anaphora) and attempts to formulate a hierarchy establishing the relationship of these forms to comprehension.

CARVER, RONALD P. "Understanding, Information Processing, and Learning from Prose Materials," *Journal of Educational Psychology*, 64 (February 1973), 76-84.

Results from this experimental data show that during comprehension of prose material, the relationship between understanding and stored information is essentially the same.

COOPER, CHARLES R. "Empirical Studies of Response to Literature: Review and Suggestions," *Journal of Aesthetic Education*, 10 (July-October 1976), 77-93.

Examines some studies of response to literature, both after reading and during reading. Suggests possibilities for future research.

FAW, HAROLD W., and T. GARY WALLER. "Mathemagenic Behaviours and Efficiency in Learning from Prose Materials: Review, Critique, and Recommendations," *Review of Educational Research*, 46, 4 (Fall 1976), 691-720.

Discusses four methods purported to improve reading comprehension: advance organizer, response modes, stated learner objectives, and question insertion. Assesses each in terms of study time, efficiency, attention, and intentional and incidental learning.

FILMER, HENRY T. "Linguistics and Reading Comprehension," *Education*, 86 (November 1965), 158-161.

Presents Piaget's developmental stages using Alfred Whithead's classifications. Relates these to linguistics and reading comprehension.

FOWLES, BARBARA, and MARCIA E. GLANZ. "Competence and Talent in Verbal Riddle Comprehension," *Journal of Child Language*, 4, 3 (October 1977), 433-452.

Experiments with children in grades one to three on tasks demanding the retelling and explaining of riddles. Finds that retelling is not related to the ability to explain the riddle. Three cognitive factors which influence riddle competence are identified and related to reading and metalinguistic development.

GARMAN, DOROTHY. "Comprehension before Word Identification," *Reading World*, 16, 4 (May 1977), 279-287.

Looks at Frank Smith's reading theory which postulates that comprehension precedes word identification. Discusses implications for reading instruction from this perspective.

GENTNER, DEDRE. *On Relational Meaning: The Acquisition of Verb Meaning*, Technical Report No. 78. Urbana-Champaign, Illinois: University of Illinois, Center for the Study of Reading, December 1977.

Discusses the acquisition of verb meanings in terms of time, components, and application.

GOLINKOFF, ROBERTA MICHNICH. "A Comparison of Reading Comprehension Processes in Good and Poor Comprehenders," *Reading Research Quarterly*, 11, 4 (1975-1976), 623-659.

Studies comprehension research for the purpose of differentiating strategies used by skilled and less skilled comprehenders. Focuses on decoding, lexical access, and text organization and examines possible interrelationships between these elements and the comprehension process.

GUTHRIE, JOHN T. (Ed.). *Cognition, Curriculum, and Comprehension*. Newark, Delaware: International Reading Association, 1977.

Presents a collection of both theoretical and practical articles on comprehension by various authors. Each article is followed by a response.

GUTHRIE, JOHN T. "Reading Comprehension and Syntactic Responses in Good and Poor Readers," *Journal of Educational Psychology*, 65 (1973), 294-299.

Shows, experimentally, that the processing of function words and verbs relies on syntax while the understanding of nouns and modifiers is determined primarily by semantics.

GUTHRIE, JOHN T. "Story Comprehension," *Reading Teacher*, 30, 5 (February 1977), 574-575, 577.

Reviews the work of Gordon Bower and Jean Mandler. Discusses story structures and comprehension processes in both children and adults.

HANSELL, T. STEVENSON. "Readability, Syntactic Transformations, and Generative Semantics," *Journal of Reading*, 19, 7 (April 1976), 557-562.

Examines readability formulas historically and describes an experiment controlling syntactic variables and the effects produced on comprehension. Concludes that there are many unknown issues of language complexity which lead to questions regarding the validity of readability formulas.

HANSON, KAREN, ROBERT SCHREINER, and THOMAS J. HUMMEL. "The Relationship between Reading Ability and Semantic Verification Tasks," in Pearson and Hansen (Eds.), *Reading: Disciplined Inquiry in Process and Practice*, Twenty-Seventh Yearbook of the National Reading Conference, 1978, 77-83.

Finds that good readers perform better on a semantic processing task than do less able readers.

HITTLEMAN, DANIEL R. "Seeking a Psycholinguistic Definition of Readability," *Reading Teacher*, 26 (May 1973), 783-789.

Describes readability as a moment in time during which the reader's experiences (cognitive, linguistic, emotional) interact with each other and with the topic, the purpose, and the text.

HUTSON, BARBARA A., and JAMES POWERS. "Reversing Irreversible Sentences: Semantic and Syntactic Factors," *Journal of Reading Behavior*, 6, 1 (April 1974), 99-110.

Studies the ability of primary youngsters to recognize probable and improbable content within active and passive sentence structures. Findings suggest that semantic development may facilitate syntactic development.

ISAKSON, RICHARD L., and JOHN W. MILLER. "Sensitivity to Syntactic and Semantic Cues in Good and Poor Comprehenders," *Journal of Educational Psychology*, 68, 6 (December 1976), 787-792.

Finds that experimental manipulations producing syntactic and semantic violations did not influence comprehension of poor readers but did cause an increase in errors for good readers.

JACKSON, MARK D., and JAMES L. McCLELLAND. "Sensory and Cognitive Determinants of Reading Speed," *Journal of Verbal Learning and Verbal Behavior*, 14, 6 (December 1975), 565-574.

Argues that faster readers ignore unrelated features and with each eye fixation are able to encode more content into memory and into higher level conceptual processing representations.

JOHNSON, RONALD E. "Meaning in Complex Learning," *Review of Educational Research*, 45, 3 (Summer 1975), 425-459.

Examines studies on the relationship of meaningfulness and the learning of verbal discourse. Emphasizes that assessments of meaningfulness now include measures of semantic and syntactic relationships and measures of referential knowledge structures.

KINGSTON, ALBERT J., and WENDELL W. WEAVER. "Recent Developments in Readability Appraisal," *Journal of Reading*, 11 (October 1967), 44-47.

Reviews the history of readability concerns and compares historical readability formulas with newer ones like the cloze procedure. Presents limitations of readability formulas.

LaBERGE, DAVID, and S. JAY SAMUELS (Eds.). *Basic Processes in Reading Perception and Comprehension*. New York: Halsted Press, 1978.

Presents writings dealing with theoretical and experimental views of perception and comprehension.

LAMB, GEORGE S., and JOHN C. TOWER. "The Portents of Reading," *Reading Teacher*, 28, 7 (April 1975), 638-642.

Applies the reading models of Goodman and Smith to practical comprehension issues. Concludes that students bring their unique experiences to the reading process and that individualized products result. Suggests some methods for classroom application.

LAYTON, PAMELA, and ADRIAN J. SIMPSON. "Surface and Deep Structure in Sentence Comprehension," *Journal of Verbal Learning and Verbal Behavior*, 14, 6 (December 1975), 658-664.

Experiments with active and passive sentence comprehension, using active and passive questions. Compares errors in terms of surface structure and deep structure retention.

MALICKY, GRACE V. "The Effect of Deletion Produced Structures on Word Identification and Comprehension of Beginning Readers" (abstract), *Reading Research Quarterly*, 12, 2 (1976-1977), 212-216.

Studies the effects of deletion transformations on word recognition and comprehension of young students. Results show that the effects are greater for comprehension than word identification; if the deletion is applied to redundant textual information, the subjects reading for meaning provided more information themselves.

MASSON, MICHAEL E.J., and LINDA S. SALA. "Interactive Processes in Sentence Comprehension and Recognition," *Cognitive Psychology*, 10, 2 (April 1978), 244-270.

Describes two experiments designed to study the effects of semantic and surface information in reading and sentence recognition. Concludes that reading and recognition are interactive processes utilizing concept and data operations; semantic and surface information also interact as parts of the comprehension and memory process.

MOIR, HUGHES. "Linguistic Factors Related to Style and Meaning in Written Language," *Elementary English*, 47 (February 1970), 215-222.

Explores the relationship between the style of written material (including phonology, syntax, and semantics) and comprehension. Cites differences between oral and written language in terms of criteria for evaluating children's reading materials and research on children's language patterns.

MYERS, MEYER, and SCOTT G. PARIS. "Children's Metacognitive Knowledge about Reading," *Journal of Educational Psychology*, 70, 5 (October 1978), 680-690.

Interviews eight and twelve year olds in regard to their knowledge about certain variables which influence reading. Results show that age-related differences in metacognitive knowledge may be correlated with certain features of reading achievement.

O'DONNEL, ROY C. "A Study of the Correlation between Awareness of Structural Relationships in English and Ability in Reading Comprehension," *Journal of Experimental Education*, 31 (March 1963), 313-316.

Investigates the relationship between reading comprehension and knowledge of grammatical structure. Finds the correlation was too low to support teaching of structure as a means to better comprehension.

OLSHAVSKY, JILL EDWARDS. "Comprehension Profiles of Good and Poor Readers across Materials of Increasing Difficulty," in Pearson and Hansen (Eds.), *Reading: Disciplined Inquiry in Process and Practice*, Twenty-Seventh Yearbook of the National Reading Conference, 1978, 73-76.

Studies the use of strategies by good and poor readers and finds that while good readers retain more strategy use, both groups use strategies less as material becomes more difficult. Postulates that the difference between good and poor readers lies not in procedure but in text difficulty.

OLSHAVSKY, JILL EDWARDS. "Reading as Problem Solving: An Investigation of Strategies," *Reading Research Quarterly*, 12, 4 (1976-1977), 654-674.

Identifies strategies employed by high and low achieving readers. Results describe a comprehension process supporting the Goodman psycholinguistic model.

PAGE, WILLIAM D. "Pseudocues, Supercues, and Comprehension," *Reading World*, 15 (May 1976), 232-238.

Investigates the predictability of post oral reading cloze comprehension from the classification of oral reading miscues as acceptable or unacceptable.

PEARSON, P. DAVID. "The Effects of Grammatical Complexity on Children's Comprehension, Recall, and Conception of Certain Semantic Relations," *Reading Research Quarterly*, 10, 2 (1974-1975), 155-192.

Discusses some linguistic variables related to reading comprehension.

PICKERT, SARAH M., and MARTHA L. CHASE. "Story Retelling: An Informal Technique for Evaluating Children's Language," *Reading Teacher*, 31, 5 (February 1978), 528-531.

Presents a simple evaluation technique for measuring children's comprehension, organization, and use of language.

POTTER, THOMAS C. *A Taxonomy of Cloze Research, Part 1: Readability and Reading Comprehension.* Inglewood, California: Southwest Regional Education Laboratory.

Reviews experimental research which has used the cloze method. Presents the most valid and reliable construction forms of cloze and makes recommendations for further research.

READENCE, JOHN E. "Cognitive Style and Oral Reading Behavior of Third Grade Children," *Reading Improvement*, 14, 3 (Fall 1977), 175-181.

Relates two types of cognitive styles, impulsive and reflective, to the type of linguistic cues a reader employs during the process of reading for meaning.

RICHEK, MARGARET ANN. "Reading Comprehension of Anaphoric Forms in Varying Linguistic Contexts," *Reading Research Quarterly*, 12, 2 (1976-1977), 145-165.

Presents paraphrasic alternations in three forms (noun, pronoun, and null) in differing linguistic contexts (varying length, kernels, parallelism, question, and sentence frame) to determine if comprehension is affected.

RUDDELL, ROBERT B. "The Effect of Oral and Written Patterns of Language Structure on Reading Comprehension," *Reading Teacher*, 18 (January 1965), 270-275.

Summarizes the author's award winning dissertation which studied the relationship of comprehension to similarity of structure between children's language and their reading material. Concludes that reading material high in low frequency patterns was harder to comprehend.

SIMONS, HERBERT D. "Reading Comprehension: The Need for a New Perspective," *Reading Research Quarterly*, 6, 3 (Spring 1971), 338-363.

Describes evaluation of reading comprehension from the perspective of seven approaches. Finds most approaches, except the psycholinguistic, relying on the inadequate standardized test. Calls for new measurement tools to be developed based on psycholinguistic theory and dealing with deep structure.

SMITH, FRANK. "Making Sense of Reading—And of Reading Instruction," *Harvard Educational Review*, 47, 3 (August 1977), 386-395.

Discusses two concepts which are essential to a child's success in reading: 1) print is meaningful and 2) speech and written language are different. Relates these two aspects of comprehension to motivation, relevancy, and instructional methods.

SMITH, FRANK. "The Role of Prediction in Reading," *Elementary English*, 52, 3 (March 1975), 305-311.

Presents a rationale for prediction in reading as a means of handling multiple word meanings, confusing spelling, and the limited processing ability of the visual and memory brain functions.

SMITH, FRANK. "The Uses of Language," *Language Arts*, 54, 6 (September 1977), 638-644.

Examines Halliday's seven functions of language and proposes three additions. Describes language acquisition and comprehension as centering around these functions.

STEFFENSEN, MARGARET, CHITRA JOGDEO, and RICHARD C. ANDERSON. *A Cross-Cultural Perspective on Reading Comprehension*, Technical Report No. 97. Urbana-Champaign, Illinois: University of Illinois, Center for the Study of Reading, July 1978.

Describes an experiment where subjects read two selections, one culturally relevant and one foreign. Results show that the relevant passage is read more rapidly and elaborated on more appropriately.

STICE, CAROLE KIRCHNER. "The Relationship between Comprehension of Oral Contrastive Stress and Silent Reading Comprehension," *Research in the Teaching of English*, 12, 2 (May 1978), 137-142.

Identifies a positive relationship between the comprehension of contrastive stress in standard English and comprehension of written language. Proposes that the child's own language be employed in reading instruction.

THEBERGE, VIVIAN E., and CARL BRAUN. "The Effect of Deletion Produced Syntactic Structures on Reading Comprehension," *Reading Horizons*, 17, 3 (Spring 1977), 183-189.

Discusses research on reading comprehension and the influence of deletion produced sentence structures. Compares the effects on reading comprehension of syntactic information in sentences with content information.

TIERNEY, ROBERT J., and JOSEPH L. VAUGHAN. "Conceptual Difficulty of Reading Materials: Identifying Conceptual Constructs for Prediction," in W. Miller and G. McNinch (Eds.), *National Reading Conference Proceedings*, 1977, 204-208.

Determines the conceptual features of a reading selection through the identification of key words, then measures the students' knowledge of the conceptual information through free association and cloze. Results show a measure of the conceptual complexity of a selection.

TOVEY, DUANE R. "Children's Perceptions of Reading," *Reading Teacher*, 29, 6 (March 1976), 536-540.

Examines children's perceptions of reading through an investigation of their concepts of 1) reading as a silent process; 2) the role of meaning; 3) the role of prediction; and 4) the operations of graphophonic, syntactic, and semantic cue systems.

VASQUEZ, CAROL A., SAM GLUCKBERG, and JOSEPH H. DANKS. "Integration of Clauses in Oral Reading: The Effects of Syntactic and Semantic

Constraints in the Eye-Voice Span," *Reading Research Quarterly*, 13, 2 (1977-1978), 174-187.

Rejects a pure syntactic-decoding model and proposes a semantic integration theory in which the rate of incoming information is controlled to coordinate with the integration of that information.

WALKER, LAURENCE. "Comprehension of Writing and Spontaneous Speech: A Comparative Study," *Visible Language*, 11, 1 (Winter 1977), 37-51.

Concludes that basic reading comprehension on a literal level involves a more exact processing of language than does listening to spontaneous speech.

WEAVER, WENDELL, et al. "Information Flow Difficulty in Relation to Reading Comprehension," *Journal of Reading Behavior*, 1 (Summer 1969), 41-49.

Discusses information processing systems in humans and attempts to relate storage and retrieval phenomena to reading comprehension.

WELLS, GORDON. "Comprehension: What It Means to Understand," *English in Education*, 10, 2 (Summer 1976), 24-36.

Argues for an expansion of the concept of comprehension to include the purposeful behavior of the comprehender and the wide range of information utilized during the comprehension process.

WHEAT, THOMAS E., and ROSE M. EDMOND. "The Concept of Comprehension: An Analysis," *Journal of Reading*, 18, 7 (April 1975), 523-527.

Draws on a psycholinguistic perspective to define comprehension in relation to the surface and deep structures of language.

WINNER, ELLEN, ANNE K. ROSENTIEL, and HOWARD GARDNER. "Language Development—Metaphoric Understanding," *Journal of Learning Disabilities*, 10, 3 (March 1977), 147-149.

Finds that metaphoric understanding is developed in a three step process.

ZINCK, R. ANN. "The Relation of Comprehension to Semantic and Syntactic Language Cues During Oral and Silent Reading," in Pearson and Hansen (Eds.), *Reading: Disciplined Inquiry in Process and Practice*, Twenty-Seventh Yearbook of the National Reading Conference, 1978, 154-160.

Compares some issues of cloze research with interpretations of miscue analysis; deals particularly with the syntactic and semantic constraints and their influence on structure and lexicon.

CURRICULUM

This section includes publications that focus on curricula in reading instruction. As fundamental as curriculum is, it is still not a major focus in the literature we've scanned.

BARRETT, THOMAS C., and DALE D. JOHNSON (Eds.). *Views on Elementary Reading Instruction.* Newark, Delaware: International Reading Association, 1973.

Presents papers about elementary reading instruction including views based on psycholinguistics and sociolinguistics; incorporation of children's thoughts, language, and actions; and affective domain and content reading.

EVANS, PETER O. "Reading as an Integrated Learning Activity," *Interchange,* 7, 4 (1976-1977), 46-52.

Calls for the integration of reading into a language communication curriculum.

GOODMAN, KENNETH S. "Behind the Eye: What Happens in Reading," in Kenneth S. Goodman and Olive S. Niles (Eds.), *Reading: Process and Program.* Champaign, Illinois: National Council of Teachers of English, 1970, 3-38.

Describes the reading process in considerable detail. Defines reading and considers how the process varies in reading different materials. Discusses implications for the reading curriculum.

GOODMAN, KENNETH S. "A Communicative Theory of the Reading Curriculum," *Elementary English,* 40 (March 1963), 290-298.

States that current reading curricula are based on knowledge of physiology, psychology, sociology, and growth and development, but not on any systematic understanding of the language itself. Presents the outlines of a curriculum that is also based on the structure of the language. States that language has a central communicative characteristic and explains how meaning is communicated in American English.

GOODMAN, YETTA M., and DOROTHY J. WATSON. "A Reading Program to Live with: Focus on Comprehension," *Language Arts*, 54, 8 (November-December 1977), 868-879.

Defends a comprehension based reading program and justifies it as being student centered, preserving holistic language and thought, and focusing on meaning.

KNIGHT, LESTER N., and CHARLES H. HARGIS. "Math Language Ability: Its Relationship to Reading in Math," *Language Arts*, 54, 4 (April 1977), 423-428.

Provides support for the position that instruction in the content area should focus on its particular language.

PAUL, ALICE. "Diverse Aspects of Language Development as Related to Reading," in M.P. Douglass (Ed.), *Claremont Reading Conference Thirty-Eighth Yearbook*. Claremont, California: 1974.

Argues that reading is an integral part of language and discusses various issues of development such as role of the teacher, the learning environment, and the child's concepts of learning and school.

SHAFER, ROBERT E. "Will Psycholinguistics Change Reading in Secondary Schools?" *Journal of Reading*, 21, 4 (January 1978), 305-316.

Supports the adoption of the psycholinguistic model of reading for the secondary curriculum.

SMITH, E. BROOKS, KENNETH S. GOODMAN, and ROBERT MEREDITH. *Language and Thinking in School*, Second Edition. New York: Holt, Rinehart and Winston, 1977.

Presents an expansion view of language development and a language centered view of the curriculum. One chapter deals with the process of reading and another with the teaching of reading.

SMITH, FRANK, and KENNETH S. GOODMAN. "On the Psycholinguistic Method of Teaching Reading," *Elementary School Journal*, 71, 4 (January 1971), 177-181.

Describes the value of psycholinguistics as it provides insights about reading to researchers and practitioners. Deplores the use of the term in connection with kits and other materials.

LANGUAGE DIFFERENCES: DIALECTS, BILINGUALISM, BILITERACY, AND SOCIOLINGUISTICS

There continues to be an interest in dialect differences and reading in the literature and interest is growing in biliteracy and reading in second languages.

AARONS, ALFRED C., BARBARA Y. GORDON, and WILLIAM A. STEWART. "Linguistics: Cultural Differences and American Education," *Florida FL Reporter*, 7 (Spring-Summer 1969).

Contains a collection of readings on linguistics and cultural differences and the implications for classroom teaching. Although few articles deal with reading, the information presented and the issues explored will be of interest to teachers of children with culturally diverse backgrounds.

BARATZ, JOAN C., and ROGER W. SHUY. *Teaching Black Children to Read*. Washington, D.C.: Center for Applied Linguistics, 1969.

Contains a collection of original and reprinted articles which present a range of positions on how reading instruction should respond to dialect differences.

CLARKE, MARK A., and SANDRA SILBERSTEIN. "Toward a Realization of Psycholinguistic Principles in the ESL Reading Class," *Language Learning*, 27, 1 (June 1977), 135-154.

Discusses psycholinguistic research in relation to the instructional framework it provides for second language learners.

CLAY, MARIE M. "Early Childhood and Cultural Diversity in New Zealand," *Reading Teacher*, 29, 4 (January 1976), 333-341.

Investigates the early reading process looking particularly at dialect and multilingual interactions of Maori, Anglo, and Samoan subjects.

CRAMER, RONALD. "Dialectology: A Case for Language Experience," *Reading Teacher*, 25, 1 (October 1971), 33-39.

Writes from the position that the more divergence there is between the language of the child and the language of the learner, the more difficult is the process of learning to read. Describes solutions to this problem and concludes that language experience is the most appropriate methodological approach.

CULLINAN, BERNICE E. (Ed.). *Black Dialects and Reading*. Urbana, Illinois: National Council of Teachers of English, Eric Clearinghouse on Reading and Communication Skills, 1974.

Discusses specific issues in reading instruction methodology for the black dialect speaker. Includes sections on diagnostic instruments, classroom strategies, grapheme-phoneme relationships, and the nature of black English.

CUNNINGHAM, PATRICIA M. "Teachers' Correction Responses to Black Dialect Miscues Which are Nonmeaning Changing," *Reading Research Quarterly*, 12, 4 (1976-1977), 637-653.

Shows that significantly more black dialect specific miscues are corrected by teachers than nondialect specific miscues.

DAVIS, A.L. (Ed.). *Culture, Class, and Language Variety: A Resource Book for Teachers*, Revised Edition. Urbana-Champaign, Illinois: National Council of Teachers of English, 1972.

Presents a collection of papers dealing with linguistic and methodological issues for culture, class, and language diversity.

DOWNING, JOHN. *Comparative Reading: Cross-National Studies of Behavior and Processes in Reading and Writing*. New York: Macmillan, 1973.

Looks at the theoretical issues of reading and language instruction from cross-national comparisons; also includes a collection of articles from various countries dealing with the state of reading and language instruction.

GOLUB, LESTER S. "Reading, Writing, and Black English," *Elementary School Journal*, 72, 4 (January 1972), 195-202.

Focuses on the child's production of language and suggests a reading and writing methodology utilizing this production.

GOODMAN, KENNETH S., and CATHERINE BUCK. "Dialect Barriers to Reading Comprehension Revisited," *Reading Teacher*, 27, 1 (October 1973), 6-12.

Suggests that black dialect speakers usually have receptive control over the standard dialect and can become proficient readers. Some reading aspects may be related to dialect but rejection of the reader's dialect must be avoided as it might lead to a failure by the readers to apply their linguistic abilities to the reading process.

GOODMAN, KENNETH S., YETTA M. GOODMAN, and BARBARA FLORES. *Reading in the Bilingual Classroom: Literacy and Biliteracy.* Rosslyn, Virginia: National Clearinghouse for Bilingual Education, 1979.

Presents a comprehensive overview about reading in bilingual education including its issues, trends, assumptions, and research. Provides a curriculum model based on current psycholinguistic research in reading for developing and expanding biliteracy.

GOODMAN, YETTA M., and RUDINE SIMS. "Whose Dialect for Beginning Readers?" *Elementary English*, 51, 6 (September 1974), 837-841.

Suggests that an examination of coping behaviors rather than special dialect readers might prove more realistic insight into reading problems.

HUDELSON, SARAH. "Children's Use of Contextual Clues in Reading Spanish," *Reading Teacher*, 30, 7 (April 1977), 735-740.

Presents cross-cultural evidence regarding the use of context in reading.

HUNT, BARBARA CAREY. "Black Dialect and Third and Fourth Graders' Performance on the Gray Oral Reading Test," *Reading Research Quarterly*, 10, 1 (1974-1975), 103-123.

Questions the scoring and interpretation on reading tests of oral reading errors related to dialect.

JOHNSON, KENNETH R. "Black Dialect Shift in Oral Reading," *Journal of Reading*, 18 (April 1975), 535-540.

Examines three types of miscues associated with black dialect and suggests how errors and translations can be distinguished.

KOLERS, PAUL A. "Reading and Talking Bilingually," *American Journal of Psychology*, 79 (September 1966), 357-376.

Adult bilingual speakers of French and English were given passages with mixed vocabulary in the two languages. Reactions of the readers to the passages reveals that grapheme-phoneme correspondences "explain nothing about comprehension." Concludes that encoding and decoding are not symmetrical operations.

LAFFEY, JAMES, and ROGER SHUY (Eds.). *Language Differences: Do They Interfere?* Newark, Delaware: International Reading Association, 1973.

Presents a collection of papers discussing the issues of language difference and learning to read.

LUCAS, MARILYN S., and HARRY SINGER. "Dialect in Relation to Oral Reading Achievement: Recoding, Encoding, or Merely a Code?" *Journal of Reading Behavior*, 7, 2 (Summer 1975), 137-138.

Offers support for the theory that dialect influences the syntactical but not the phonological level of oral reading.

NICHOLS, PATRICIA C. "A Sociolinguistic Perspective on Reading and Black Children," *Language Arts*, 54, 2 (February 1977), 150-157.

Summarizes the debate over dialect differences and interference with reading and submits evidence, from field work conducted in rural South Carolina schools, that linguistics and social factors are of equal importance in reading.

RIGG, PAT. "Dialect and/in/for Reading," *Language Arts*, 55, 3 (March 1978), 285-290.

Describes eye dialects and suggests techniques which help avoid miscues caused by this phenomena.

RYSTROM, RICHARD. "Caveat Qui Credit (Let the Believer Beware)," *Journal of Reading*, 16, 3 (December 1972), 236-240.

Questions the typical stereotypes and generalizations of black dialect such as the supposed causal relationships between dialect and performance and the supposed smaller vocabularies of black children.

SIMONS, HERBERT D., and KENNETH R. JOHNSON. "Black English Syntax and Reading Interference," *Research in the Teaching of English*, 8, 3 (Winter 1975), 339-358.

Investigates the relationship between reading achievement of black students and grammatical interference. Concludes that there is no significant relationship.

SMITHERMAN, GENEVA. "Grammar and Goodness," *English Journal*, 62 (May 1973), 774-778.

Examines the linguistic purist position as being related to racism and classism. Discusses the need for the description of black dialect and for teachers to focus on communication skills.

SOMERVILL, MARY ANN, and JOHN F. JACOBS. "The Use of Dialect in Reading Materials for Black Innercity Children," *Negro Educational Review*, 23, 1 (January 1972), 13-23.

Finds that children read and comprehend dialect better than standard English.

STEWART, WILLIAM A. "Current Issues in the Use of Negro Dialect in Beginning Reading Texts," *Florida FL Reporter*, Spring/Fall 1970, 3-7.

Describes the background of dialect use in textbooks and examines some current concerns about the use of such readers.

TANG, BENITA T. "A Psycholinguistic Study of the Relationships between Children's Ethnic-Linguistic Attitudes and the Effectiveness of Methods Used in Second Language Reading Instruction," *TESOL Quarterly*, 8, 3 (September 1974), 233-251.

Looks at the attitudes of children concerning their native and second languages. Discusses these attitudes in terms of the translation methodology.

VENEZKY, RICHARD L. "Nonstandard Language and Reading," *Elementary English*, 47 3 (March 1970), 334-345.

Discusses the use of various instructional approaches being used for nonstandard English speakers, emphasizing beginning reading and the language of the reading materials. Includes a comprehensive bibliography.

WALKER, L. "Newfoundland Dialect and Interference in Oral Reading," *Journal of Reading Behavior*, 7 (1975), 61-78.

Examines Newfoundland dialect speakers to determine if syntactical differences affect oral reading performance.

ZIROS, GAIL I. "Language Interference and Teaching the Chicano to Read," *Journal of Reading*, 19, 4 (January 1976), 284-288.

Suggests that the Chicano's bilingualism does not cause interference in language. Proposes that if there are difficulties, semantics needs to be emphasized and not phonology or morphology.

ZUCK, LOUIS V., and YETTA M. GOODMAN. *Social Class and Regional Dialects: Their Relationship to Reading*, an annotated bibliography. Newark, Delaware: International Reading Association, 1971.

Presents an extensive bibliography of articles dealing with social, regional, and ethnic dialects as they relate to the teaching and learning of reading.

DISCOURSE ANALYSIS

Discourse analysis, the analysis of whole connected language texts, is growing rapidly as an area of concern. A number of alternate analytic systems have emerged and the literature is rich in controversy. Discourse analysis is becoming an area of great interest among cognitive psychologists building on work done many years ago by Bartlett, the British psychologist. Work in artificial intelligence using computers also has been focused on analysis of discourse.

ANDERSON, RICHARD C., RAND J. SPIRO, and WILLIAM E. MONTAGUE (Eds.). *Schooling and the Acquisition of Knowledge.* Hillsdale, New Jersey: Lawrence Erlbaum Associates, 1977.

Presents the results of a conference which focused on schooling and the acquisition of knowledge. Papers are diverse but possess commonality in the position that a person's current state of knowledge influences what will be gained from educational sources.

ANDERSON, RICHARD C., RAND J. SPIRO, and MARK C. ANDERSON. "Schemata as Scaffolding for the Representation of Information in Connected Discourse," *American Education Research Journal,* 15, 3 (Summer 1978), 433-440.

Uses the same information in two different contextual settings to test the effect of schemata on recall.

BARTLETT, F.C. *Remembering: A Study in Experimental and Social Psychology.* London: Cambridge University Press, 1932.

Introduces many of the issues which are currently being examined in discourse analysis.

BERGER, NATALIE S., and CHARLES A. PERFETTI. "Reading Skill and Memory for Spoken and Written Discourse," *Journal of Reading Behavior,* 9, 1 (Spring 1977), 7-16.

Compares memory performances after participation in a reading-listening exercise. Results indicate that listening and reading comprehension are both processed in the same way and that individual differences are apparent in the way units are organized into relationships.

BRIDGE, CONNIE, ROBERT TIERNEY, and MARY JANE CERA. "Inferential Operations of Children Involved in Discourse Processing," in Pearson and Hansen (Eds.), *Reading: Disciplined Inquiry in Process and Practice*, Twenty-Seventh Yearbook of the National Reading Conference, 1978, 68-72.

Finds children making inferences in recall for even the most basic stories. Concludes that comprehension is one process for both proficient and nonproficient readers.

DOOLING, D. JAMES, and REBECCA L. MULLET. "Locus of Thematic Effects in Retention of Prose," *Journal of Experimental Psychology*, 97, 3 (March 1973), 404-406.

Describes an experiment in which the story theme is used as a mnemonic device. Finds that under certain conditions it facilitates recall.

FREDERIKSEN, CARL H. "Acquisition of Semantic Information from Discourse: Effects of Repeated Exposure," *Journal of Verbal Learning and Verbal Behavior*, 14, 2 (April 1975), 158-169.

Tests the conceptual and relational responses of listening recall. Concludes that processes of adjustment occur between periods of information acquisition and information recall.

GARROD, SIMON, and ANTHONY SANFORD. "Interpreting Anaphoric Relations: The Integration of Semantic Information While Reading," *Journal of Verbal Learning and Verbal Behavior*, 16, 1 (February 1977), 77-90.

Describes four experiments dealing with the integration of semantic information and proposes a theoretical model of textual comprehension.

GLENN, CHRISTINE G. "The Role of Episodic Structure and of Story Length in Children's Recall of Simple Stories," *Journal of Verbal Learning and Verbal Behavior*, 17, 2 (April 1978), 229-247.

Examines and discusses the results of second graders' recall of story in terms of the variables of length and episodic structure.

GOETZ, ERNEST. *Sentences in Lists and in Connected Discourse*, Technical Report 3. Urbana-Champaign, Illinois: Laboratory for Cognitive Studies in Education, November 1975.

Offers a probing examination of the work to date on experimentation involving sentences or connected text.

JUST, MARCEL ADAM, and PATRICIA CARPENTER. *Cognitive Processes in Comprehension*. Hillsdale, New Jersey: Lawrence Erlbaum Associates, 1977.

Presents studies which examine the processing of thought involved in listening to a conversation or reading a selection.

KIERAS, DAVID E. "Good and Bad Structure in Simple Paragraphs: Effects on Apparent Theme, Reading Time, and Recall," *Journal of Verbal Learning and Verbal Behavior*, 17, 1 (February 1978), 13-28.

Examines subjects' processing of traditional paragraph structure by looking at reading performance in confirming and nonconfirming selections.

KINTSCH, W., and others. "Comprehension and Recall of Text as a Function of Content Variable," *Journal of Verbal Learning and Verbal Behavior*, 14, 2 (April 1975), 196-214.

Presents experiments on the influence of varying the number of word concepts in the text, keeping the number of words and propositions controlled. Finds that with more word concepts, the time involved in reading is longer and the amount recalled is less.

KINTSCH, WALTER. *The Representation of Meaning in Memory*. Hillsdale, New Jersey: Lawrence Erlbaum Associates, 1974.

Discusses comprehension in relation to discourse analysis.

KLEIMAN, GLENN, and DIANE SCHALLERT. "Some Things the Reader Needs to Know that the Listener Doesn't," in Pearson and Hansen (Eds.), *Reading: Disciplined Inquiry in Process and Practice*, Twenty-Seventh Yearbook of the National Reading Conference, 1978, 138-142.

Looks at the differences and not at the similarities between listening and reading. Includes topics on intonation, situation, functions, syntax, redundancy, and permanence.

MALGADY, ROBERT. "Discriminant Analysis of Psychological Judgments of Literal and Figurative Meaningfulness and Anomaly," *Journal of Psychology*, 95 (March 1977), 217-221.

Regards literal, figurative, and anomalous sentences as components of a language use continuum. Opposes the traditional view of qualitative difference.

MANDLER, JEAN M., and NANCY S. JOHNSON. "Remembrance of Things Parsed: Story Structure and Recall," *Cognitive Psychology*, 9, 1 (January 1977), 111-151.

Studies story structure schemata in children and adults and concludes that story schemata are developmental and contribute to recall differences.

MARSCHARK, MARC, and ALLAN PAIVIO. "Integrative Processing of Concrete and Abstract Sentences," *Journal of Verbal Learning and Verbal Behavior*, 16, 2 (April 1977), 217-231.

Suggests that both concrete and abstract sentences are processed holistically with the construction of mental representations based on contextual information, linguistic knowledge, and general knowledge.

MEYER, BONNIE J.F. "Identification of the Structure of Prose and Its Implications for the Study of Reading and Memory," *Journal of Reading Behavior*, 11, 1 (1975), 7-47.

Provides an introduction to the field of text analysis.

ORTONY, ANDREW, and others. "Interpreting Metaphors and Idioms: Some Effects of Context on Comprehension," *Journal of Verbal Learning and Verbal Behavior*, 17, 4 (August 1978), 465-477.

Experiments with the establishment of a contextual expectation and its effects on reaction time for understanding subsequent sentences. Finds that similar processes seem to be required for the comprehension of figurative and literal language.

PITKIN, WILLIS L., JR. "X/Y: Some Basic Strategies of Discourse," *College English*, 38, 7 (March 1977), 660-672.

Illustrates the concept of a hierarchical model of discourse by presenting a set of binary relations.

REDER, LYNNE M. *Comprehension and Retention of Prose: A Literature Review*, Technical Report No. 108. Urbana-Champaign, Illinois: University of Illinois, Center for the Study of Reading, November 1978.

Discusses an author's intentions in terms of implicit and explicit text. Makes recommendations for comprehension improvement involving use of inference, elaboration of important text, and background knowledge of conceptual references.

RUBIN, ANN D., BERTRAM BRUCE, and JOHN S. BROWN. *A Process-Oriented Language for Describing Aspects of Reading Comprehension*, Technical Report No. 13. Urbana-Champaign, Illinois: University of Illinois, Center for the Study of Reading, October, 1976.

Describes the development of a reading comprehension language to facilitate test construction, develop instructional materials, and conduct research studies. The possibilities of this language will be examined through the design and use of a computer model of comprehension for a specific text.

STEIN, NANCY L. *How Children Understand Stories: A Developmental Analysis*, Technical Report No. 69. Urbana-Champaign, Illinois: University of Illinois, Center for the Study of Reading, March 1978.

Discusses the application of a story grammar approach to comprehension. Presents studies which confirm the validity of this method.

THORNDYKE, PERRY W. "The Role of Inferences in Discourse Comprehension," *Journal of Verbal Learning and Verbal Behavior*, 15, 4 (August 1976), 437-446.

Studies the role of inference in reading and how it contributes to the understanding of text.

THORNDYKE, PERRY W. "Cognitive Structures in Comprehension and Memory of Narrative Discourse," *Cognitive Psychology*, 9, 1 (January 1977), 77-110.

Describes two experiments designed to evaluate the influence of structure and content variables on comprehension and memory of prose passages.

WATERS, HARRIET SALATAS. "Superordinate-Subordinate Structure in Semantic Memory: The Roles of Comprehension and Retrieval Processes," *Journal of Verbal Learning and Verbal Behavior*, 17, 5 (October 1978), 587-597.

Applies Kintsch's model to an analysis of propositions in passages subjects will be asked to recall. Finds that high-order propositions are consistently recalled more often even across age groupings. Finds evidence to support the superordinate-subordinate structure theory.

GENERAL APPLICATIONS OF LINGUISTICS AND PSYCHOLINGUISTICS TO READING

These selections are broad applications to reading as well as longer texts that deal with the entire field.

DOUGLASS, MALCOLM P. (Ed.). *Reading in Education: A Broader View.* Columbus, Ohio: Charles E. Merrill, 1973.

Presents selections from the Claremont Reading Conferences, 1963-1971. Among the topics covered are psycholinguistics, sociolinguistics, the issues of immediacy and relevancy to teaching, the place of reading in the curriculum, and acceptance of dialect.

FISHBEIN, JUSTIN, and ROBERT EMANS. *A Question of Competence: Language, Intelligence, and Learning to Read.* Chicago: Science Research Associates, 1972.

Asks the reader to examine the nature of the learner in terms of mind and language. Discusses the development of competence in thought, language, and reading primarily using the work of Piaget, Lenneberg, Chomsky, Vygotsky, and Underwood.

FRIES, CHARLES C. *Linguistics and Reading.* New York: Holt, Rinehart and Winston, 1964.

Presents a scholarly review of the history of reading instruction, a nontechnical review of descriptive linguistics (available as a separate paperback), and the author's own model of reading instruction. This last is based on minimal contrasts of spelling patterns. In linguistic terms, it is a morphophonemic rather than a phonemic approach. The child learns to associate graphic sequences with sound sequences.

GIBSON, ELEANOR J., and HARRY LEVIN. *The Psychology of Reading.* Cambridge, Massachusetts: The MIT Press, 1975.

Represents a theoretical viewpoint that higher-level cognitive processes such as rule formation, discovery of order, and selection of information, are involved in reading. Critiques models and concludes reading models are multiple.

GIORDANO, GERARD. "Convergent Research on Language and Teaching Reading," *Exceptional Children*, 44, 8 (May 1978), 604-610.

Addresses itself to the needs of special education through a review of research from the fields of developmental linguistics, linguistics, and neuropsychology.

GOODMAN, KENNETH S. "The Linguistics of Reading," *Elementary School Journal*, 64 (April 1964), 355-361.

Contends that early linguistic approaches to reading by Bloomfield, Fries, and Henry Lee Smith drew only on phonemics and were not complete by linguistic or pedagogic standards. Calls for integration of linguistic knowledge with existing psychological, sociological, physiological, and educational knowledge to produce a new synthesis. States that the educator must play the central role in this process.

GOODMAN, KENNETH S., and JAMES FLEMING (Eds.). *Psycholinguistics and the Teaching of Reading*. Newark, Delaware: International Reading Association, 1969.

Presents papers on reading issues discussed from a psycholinguistic perspective. Articles include examinations of the issues of visual cues, spelling, words and morphemes, language and cultural differences, comprehension, communication model development, linguistics and reading, and beginning reading.

HENDERSON, EDMUND H. "Reading Is Not Decoding," *Reading World*, 17, 3 (March 1978), 244-249.

Discusses the relationship of reading and language development. Suggests that children's increasing discrimination abilities correlate with stages on conceptual reorganization.

HITTELMAN, DANIEL R. *Developmental Reading: A Psycholinguistic Perspective*. Chicago: Rand McNally College Publishing Company, 1978.

Presents a theoretical rationale, based on current research, which provides a framework for initiating instructional strategies.

HOLDAWAY, DON. *The Foundatons of Literacy*. Gosford, N.S.W., Australia: Ashton Scholastic, 1979.

Explores a variety of ways in which teachers can help children become literate. Outlines a hypothesis, discusses the theories involved, explores the implications for the classroom, and provides practical applications for the teacher in each section of this book.

HUEY, EDMUND. *Psychology and Pedagogy of Reading.* Cambridge, Massachusetts: MIT Press, 1968.

Reprints this classic turn of the century text which raised insights about the reading process that seem almost contemporary.

JONES, MARGARET H. "Some Thoughts on Perceptual Units in Language Processing," in Kenneth S. Goodman (Ed.), *The Psycholinguistic Nature of the Reading Process.* Detroit, Michigan: Wayne State University, 1968, 41-57.

Reviews extensive research on units in language processing and offers the author's own conclusions.

KINGSTON, ALBERT J. (Ed.). *Toward a Psychology of Language and Reading: Selected Papers of Wendell W. Weaver.* Athens, Georgia: University of Georgia Press, 1977.

Views reading as part of language and cognition, and incorporates a communications model. The cloze technique is used as a research method.

KOLERS, PAUL A. "Experiments in Reading," *Scientific American,* 22, 7 (July 1972), 84-92.

Suggests that reading is not a linear function but that more divergent processes are involved in the forming of hypotheses.

KOLERS, PAUL A. "Reading Temporally and Spatially Transformed Texts," in Kenneth S. Goodman (Ed.), *The Psycholinguistic Nature of the Reading Process.* Detroit, Michigan: Wayne State University Press, 1968, 27-40.

Reports experiments conducted by the author which required adult subjects to read passages in which the print was distorted in a variety of ways.

LEE, DORRIS M., and JOSEPH B. RUBIN. *Children and Language.* Belmont, California: Wadsworth, 1979.

Emphasizes the value of building a language arts program based on each child's natural development of language learning. Suggests many practical experiences for classroom use.

LeFEVRE, CARL A. "A Comprehensive Linguistic Approach to Reading," *Elementary English*, 42 (October 1965), 651-659.

Argues for a synthesis of many views to produce a linguistically valid system of reading instruction. Discusses Bloomfield and Fries and Lefevre's own sentence approach.

LeFEVRE, CARL A. *Linguistics and the Teaching of Reading.* New York: McGraw-Hill, 1964.

Presents a view of linguistics and reading which makes the sentence the focal point and puts great stress on intonation and syntax. Words and phoneme-grapheme correspondences are not important in LeFevre's approach.

LIPTON, AARON. "Reading Behavior of Children with Emotional Problems: A Psycholinguistic Perspective," *Reading World*, 15, 1 (October 1975), 10-22.

Calls for more research determining the relationship between psychodynamic and psycholinguistic theories as applied to pupil-teacher interactions in working with children with emotional and reading difficulties.

LOBAN, WALTER. *Language Development: Kindergarten through Grade Twelve.* Urbana, Illinois: National Council of Teachers of English, 1976.

Reports a longitudinal study of language development in a group of west coast children who were followed from kindergarten through high school. Fresh approaches to language study characterize this research. A number of conclusions relate to reading and language development.

MAVROGENES, NANCY A. "Using Psycholinguistic Knowledge to Improve Secondary Reading," *Journal of Reading*, 18, 4 (January 1975), 280-286.

Suggests applications of psycholinguistic knowledge for the reading improvement of secondary students.

MOUNTFORD, JOHN. "Some Psycholinguistic Components of Initial Standard Literacy," *Journal of Typographic Research*, 4 (Autumn 1970), 295-306.

Presents a psycholinguistic view of literacy and acquisition of literacy within a broad linguistic framework. Contrasts acquisition of "linguacy" in its initial form, "articulacy" (oral language), with extension of linguacy to a second language and to a second medium, literacy. Establishes contrasts between literate and nonliterate language users.

NILSEN, DON L.F., and ALLEEN PACE NILSEN. *Semantic Theory: A Linguistic Perspective*. Rowley, Massachusetts: Newbury House, 1975.

Provides comprehensive and current information about issues in the field of semantics to linguists and language teachers.

PAGE, WILLIAM D. "The Author and the Reader in Writing and Reading," *Research in the Teaching of English*, 8, 2 (Fall 1974), 170-183.

Examines the intentions of author and reader in studying the interrelations of reading and writing as communications.

SMITH, FRANK. *Understanding Reading: A Psycholinguistic Analysis of Reading and Learning to Read*, Second Edition. New York: Holt, Rinehart and Winston, 1978.

Advances a reading theory built on psycholinguistics, psychology, and information theory. Contends that reading is characterized by a continuous attempt to "reduce uncertainty." Identifying letters or words involves tasks different from searching for meaning and requires the reader to use more information than is otherwise needed.

WARDHAUGH, RONALD. *Reading: A Linguistic Perspective*. New York: Harcourt Brace Jovanovich, 1969.

Brings linguistics to focus on reading and the teaching of reading. Although Wardhaugh writes from the vantage point of generative-transformational linguistics, he assumes no prior knowledge of linguistics in his readers. He, therefore, provides a thorough if rapid background before he presents a broadscale application to reading.

WEBER, ROSE-MARIE. *Linguistics and Reading*. Washington, D.C.: Center for Applied Linguistics, 1970.

Gives an overview of the aspects of linguistics which have been brought to bear on the knowledge of child language and the relationship between spoken and written language. Explores how these relate to the teaching of reading and the reading process.

WILKINSON, ANDREW. *The Foundations of Language: Talking and Reading to Young Children.* New York: Oxford University Press, 1971.

Gives an overview and introduction to the field of psycholinguistics and discusses early childhood experiences from a linguistic perspective.

INSTRUCTION IN READING

Selections in this section focus on the teaching and learning of reading rather than on the reading process.

ALLEN, P. DAVID. "Cue Systems Available During the Reading Process: A Psycholinguistic Viewpoint," *Elementary School Journal*, 72, 5 (February 1972), 258-264.

Approaches the teaching of reading instruction from the viewpoint that the child's strengths need to be determined and applied to the reading process.

APPLEBEE ARTHUR N. "Writing and Reading," *Journal of Reading*, 20, 6 (March 1977), 534-537.

Looks at the research relating to reading and writing, particularly from the focus of identifying the factors which promote the positive effect of practice in one area producing improvement in the other.

BLOOMFIELD, LEONARD, and CLARENCE BARNHART. *Let's Read: A Linguistic Approach*. Detroit: Wayne State University Press, 1962.

Presents Barnhart's edited and published material developed by Bloomfield decades earlier. Bloomfield, drawing entirely on phonemics, wanted to teach grapheme-phoneme correspondences by presenting one syllable words in which the relationships were regular (one to one). Meaning was unimportant in his system. Includes Bloomfield's *Elementary English Review* articles, published in 1942.

BOND, GUY L., and ROBERT DYKSTRA. "The Cooperative Research Program in First Grade Reading Instruction," *Reading Research Quarterly*, 2 (Summer 1967).

Presents thirty comparative studies of reading methods, some of which deal with programs labeled linguistic. These programs all use phoneme-grapheme correspondence or spelling patterns as a major focus.

BRUNETTI GERALD J. "The Bullock Report: Some Implications for American Teachers and Parents," *English Journal*, 67, 8 (November 1978), 58-64.

Discusses the Bullock Report's implications for American teachers and urges its implementation.

CALFEE, ROBERT C., and RICHARD L. VENEZKY. "Component Skills in Beginning Reading," in Kenneth S. Goodman and James T. Fleming (Eds.), *Psycholinguistics and the Teaching of Reading*. Newark, Delaware: International Reading Association, 1969, 91-110.

Reports a search for component skills and variables that would predict success in reading. Concludes that the tests commonly used in reading readiness and achievement were basically inadequate.

CARROLL, JOHN B. "Some Neglected Relationships in Reading and Language Learning," *Elementary English*, 43 (October 1966), 577-582.

Poses the question, "Since children master all essential parts of their native language by age six or seven, is it possible for children to learn to read in the same natural way?" Carroll then compares and contrasts learning to read and learning the native language. He suggests that reading instruction should alternate between periods of carefully controlled sequences and periods in which the natural language of the text should be presented.

CHOMSKY, CAROL. "After Decoding, What?" *Language Arts*, 53, 3 (March 1976), 288-296, 314.

Describes a method for promoting reading using tape recordings of a variety of books.

COMBS, WARREN E. "Sentence-Combining Practice Aids Reading Comprehension," *Journal of Reading*, 21, 1 (October 1977), 18-24.

Presents an instructional method for sentence combining which is claimed to improve reading comprehension and also cites studies which provide a research base for this position.

DOWNING, JOHN. "An Application of the Comparative Method to a Practical Education Problem: Literacy Learning," *School Review*, 83, 3 (May 1975), 449-459.

Examines the influences of culture on learning and presents the results of cross-national research from fourteen countries. Issues explored include the value of being literate, sex roles in the acquisition of reading, cultural priorities, and psycholinguistic factors.

EMANS, ROBERT. "Oral Language and Learning to Read," *Elementary English*, 50 (September 1973), 929-934.

Calls for an instructional reading program based on the inherent natural way in which children learn.

ESTES, THOMAS H., and JULIE P. JOHNSTONE. "Twelve Easy Ways to Make Readers Hate Reading (And One Difficult Way to Make Them Love It)," *Language Arts*, 54, 8 (November-December 1977), 891-897.

Discusses twelve classroom reading practices and their negative effects on reading achievement.

FOERSTER, LEONA M. "Language Experience for Dialectically Different Black Learners," *Elementary English*, 51, 2 (February 1974), 193-197.

Presents support for using a language experience approach with black dialect speakers.

FROESE, VICTOR. "How to Cause Word-by-Word Reading," *Reading Teacher*, 30, 6 (March 1977), 611-615.

Discusses examples of teachers' lack of knowledge of young children's language and thought processes which contribute to instructional errors in reading.

GIBSON, ELEANOR J. "Learning to Read," in Harry Singer and Robert Ruddell (Eds.), *Theoretical Models and Processes in Reading*. Newark, Delaware: International Reading Association, 1970, 315-334.

Presents a theory of learning to read which assumes three phases: 1) learning to differentiate graphic symbols, 2) learning to decode letters to sounds, and 3) using progressively high order units of structure. Experimental studies on these phases are described.

GOURLEY, JUDITH W. "This Basal Is Easy to Read—Or Is It?" *Reading Teacher*, 32, 2 (November 1978), 174-182.

Questions the simplified language used in basals, particularly looking at pronouns, articles, and passives. Suggests that its unnaturalness often makes reading more difficult and that decisions regarding the inclusion of materials in basals are made with limited application of knowledge of children's language and the reading process.

GOWIE, CHERYL J. "Psycholinguistic Strategies for Improving Reading Comprehension," *Elementary School Journal*, 72, 2, 67-73.

Connects research in reading comprehension with instruction in the classroom, emphasizing the interaction process between reader and text which serves to develop the reader's understanding. Focuses on three areas: comprehension and reader expectations, the role of knowledge structures, and reading as a dialectic process.

GUTKNECHT, BRUCE, and DONNA KEENAN. "Basic Skills: Not Which, but Why, and an Enlightened How," *Reading Teacher*, 31, 6 (March 1978), 668-674.

Emphasizes that the way to more productive teaching is through a knowledge base of the relationship between language and reading, not through the use of a list of basic skills.

HALL, MARYANNE. "Linguistically Speaking, Why Language Experience?" *Reading Teacher*, 25, 4 (January 1972), 328-331.

Presents a broad linguistic rationale for the use of the language experience approach with beginning readers. Includes a discussion of reading and communication, oral language, writing, language patterns, meaningful language units, and oral expression.

HALL, MARYANNE, and JERILYN K. RIBOVICH. "Teach Reading in Reading Situations," *Reading Teacher*, 27 (November 1973), 163-166.

Recommends the whole language approach for reading instruction and gives some practical suggestions to teachers for viewing skills instruction holistically.

HOSKISSON, KENNETH. "The Many Facets of Assisted Reading," *Elementary English*, 52, 3 (March 1975), 312-315.

Describes the assisted reading process and discusses its applications at home and in school.

JENKINSON, MARION D. "Serendipity or System in Developing Independent Readers," *Elements: Translating Theory Into Practice*, 7, 1 (September 1975), 1-6.

Theorizes about the cognitive and linguistic aspects of reading comprehension and gives applications for the development of teaching methods.

JOHNS, JERRY L. "Strategies for Oral Reading Behavior," *Language Arts*, 52, 8 (November-December 1975), 1104-1107.

Uses the Goodman and Burke Reading Miscue Inventory as a base for providing reading instruction strategies.

LORENZ, ESTELLE. "Excuse Me but Your Idiom Is Showing," *Reading Teacher*, 31, 1 (October 1977), 24-27.

Offers suggestions for the introduction of figurative speech and idioms in the language arts program.

MALMSTROM, JEAN. "Psycholinguistics and Reading," *Elementary English*, 52, 3 (March 1975), 316-319.

Emphasizes that beginning readers be encouraged to use context and be given the freedom to guess at unknown words, using the text for confirmation.

MARTIN, NANCY. "Encounters with 'Models'," *English in Education*, 10, 1 (Spring 1976), 9-15.

Emphasizes that models play a crucial part in the acquisition of literacy.

MENOSKY, DOROTHY, and KENNETH S. GOODMAN. "Unlocking the Program," *Instructor*, 80 (March 1971), 44-46.

Presents the need for teaching reading within the context of natural language. Rejects the concept of teaching from part to whole in reading.

OLSEN, HANS C., JR. "Linguistics and Material for Beginning Reading Instruction," in Kenneth S. Goodman (Ed.), *The Psycholinguistic Nature of the Reading Process*. Detroit: Wayne State University Press, 1968, 271-287.

Examines several programs for teaching reading which claim to be based on linguistics, use linguistics knowledge, or employ a linguistic method. Olsen attempts to assess the validity and meaning of these claims.

PEARSON, P. DAVID, and DALE D. JOHNSON. *Teaching Reading Comprehension*. New York: Holt, Rinehart and Winston, 1978.

Presents principles for teachers to apply to reading instruction based on an integration of practical and theoretical knowledge.

PEARSON, P. DAVID, and MICHAEL L. KAMIL. *Basic Processes and Instructional Practices in Teaching Reading*, Reading Educational Report No. 7. Urbana-Champaign, Illinois: University of Illinois, Center for the

Study of Reading, December 1978.

Examines the need for a theoretical base in regard to instructional decisions and classifies reading theories as top/down, bottom/up, and interactive. Looks at some areas of controversy—initial program emphasis, subskills, sequencing, practice, miscues—and indicates how the theories apply to each area.

PEHRSSON, R. "The Effects of Teacher Interference During the Process of Reading or How Much of a Helper is Mr. Gelper?" *Journal of Reading*, 17, 8 (1974), 617-621.

Examines the effects of teacher intervention during reading in terms of interference with meaning, speed, and reader independence.

PIKULSKI, JOHN J. "Linguistics Applied to Reading Instruction," *Language Arts*, 53, 4 (April 1976), 373-377, 384.

Applies the work from linguistics and psycholinguistics to classroom reading instruction.

PINNELL, GAY S. "Language in Primary Classrooms," *Theory into Practice*, 14 (December 1975), 318-327.

Indicates that a language development program must attend to the function of language as well as its form.

REED, DAVID W. "A Glance at the Linguistic Organizations of Elementary Reading Textbooks," in Doris V. Gunderson (Compiler), *Language and Reading: An Interdisciplinary Approach*. Washington, D.C.: Center for Applied Linguistics, 1970.

Categorizes reading textbooks into four types and finds a lack of the whole language approach.

RENTAL, VICTOR M., and FRANK J. ZIDONIS. "Discovering Reading," *Theory into Practice*, 14, 3 (June 1975), 166-172.

Discusses the reading process as being a part of language and discusses the implications this has for teaching. Also focuses on the relationship of conceptual growth and reading.

ROTHKOPF, ERNST Z. "Writing to Teach and Reading to Learn: A Perspective on the Psychology of Written Instruction," *The Psychology of Teaching Methods*, Seventy-Fifth Yearbook of the National Society for the Study of Education, Part I. Chicago: University of Chicago Press, 1976, 91-129.

Presents a process model for textual comprehension which describes reading behaviors. Offers suggestions for control of behaviors and gives a summary of related research.

SCHWARTZ, JUDY I. "A Language Experience Approach to Beginning Reading," *Elementary English*, 52, 3 (March 1975), 320-324.

Indicates that the best way to find a beginning point for reading instruction is to look at the students themselves.

SMITH, ALEX. "The Language Context of Reading and Learning to Read in the Primary School," *Reading*, 11, 1 (April 1977), 13-19.

Declares that teacher training programs need to stress children's total language experiences and that reading should be taught within a total language context.

SPENCER, MARGARET. "Understanding Children Reading," *Times Educational Supplement*. London: No. 3185, June 18, 1976, 18-19.

Looks at the work of Jane Torrey and Margaret Clark and discusses the educational contributions of this new research in regard to our knowledge of how children learn to read.

STANSELL, JOHN, JEROME HARSTE, and ROGER DeSANTI. "The Effects of Differing Materials on the Reading Process," in Pearson and Hansen (Eds.), *Reading: Disciplined Inquiry in Process and Practice*, Twenty-Seventh Yearbook of the National Reading Conference, 1978, 27-35.

Finds that the reading process is much the same across various content area materials. Instruction should emphasize the cueing systems provided by language and facilitate student use of these cues.

TAYLOR, JoELLYN. "Making Sense: The Basic Skill in Reading," *Language Arts*, 54, 6 (September 1977), 668-672.

Presents the view that students should be focusing on meaning and not on mechanics.

TAYLOR, NANCY E., and JACQUELYN M. VAWTER. "Helping Children Discover the Functions of Written Language," *Language Arts*, 55, 8 (November-December 1978), 941-945.

Operates from Halliday's and Smith's language functions to discuss the importance of children learning and understanding the functions of written language.

TOVEY, DUANE R. "The Psycholinguistic Guessing Game," *Language Arts*, 53 (March 1976), 319-322.

Builds on children's own knowledge of linguistics to promote the use of syntactic and semantic cues during reading. Gives illustration of the use of language experience stories to build strategies.

TOVEY, DUANE R. "Improving Children's Comprehension Abilities," *Reading Teacher*, 30, 3 (December 1976), 288-292.

Discusses the linguistic, psycholinguistic, and psychological aspects of comprehension. Provides suggestions for teachers to use in evaluating comprehension activities.

MISCUE ANALYSIS

Analysis of the unexpected responses of oral readers, miscue analysis, has continued to be a popular concern in research and in teacher education.

ALLEN, P. DAVID, and DOROTHY J. WATSON. *Findings of Research in Miscue Analysis: Classroom Applications.* Urbana-Champaign, Illinois: National Council of Teachers of English, 1976.

Contains a series of articles on research done in miscue analysis and the application of same in the classroom.

BEAN, THOMAS W. "Decoding Strategies of Hawaiian Islands Dialect Speakers in Grades Four, Five, and Six," *Reading World*, 17, 4 (May 1978), 295-305.

Discusses decoding strategies employed by Hawaiian dialect speakers evaluated by the Reading Miscue Inventory.

BEAVER, JOSEPH C. "Transformational Grammar and the Teaching of Reading," *Research in the Teaching of English*, 2 (Fall 1968), 161-171.

Presents a "look-think-reproduce" theory of reading based on examination of children's reading errors. Concludes that many children's reading errors prove that the process of reading involves the whole grammatical process.

BEEBE, M.J. "Case Studies of Grade Level Effects on Children's Miscues and Reading Comprehension," *Canadian Journal of Education*, 1, 2 (1976), 51-62.

Examines the interactions of grades two and four pupils with reading materials; the Reading Miscue Inventory is used for the analysis. The focus is on the discovery of differences in interaction between grade levels and the determination of the extent to which different miscues affect comprehension.

BROWN, VIRGINIA (Ed.). "Programs, Materials, and Techniques: Reading Miscue Analysis," *Journal of Reading Disabilities*, 8, 10 (December 1975), 605-611.

Addresses itself to the area of learning disabilities. Reviews some material from this perspective including the Goodman/Burke Reading Miscue Inventory.

BURKE, CAROLYN, and KENNETH GOODMAN. "When a Child Reads: A Psycholinguistic Analysis," *Elementary English*, 47 (January 1970), 121-129.

Illustrates through the detailed analysis of one fourth grade child's oral reading miscues how such analysis can reveal the reading process at work.

BURKE, ELIZABETH. "A Development Study of Children's Reading Strategies," *Educational Review*, 29, 1 (November 1976), 30-46.

Looks at children's miscues across age and finds that, in general, miscues are of a higher quality in older children. Use of semantics shows the greatest improvement.

DANK, MARIAN. "What Effect Do Reading Programs Have on the Oral Reading Behavior of Children?" *Reading Improvement*, 14, 2 (Summer 1977), 66-69.

Analyzes the reading miscues of twenty children using the Reading Miscue Inventory and finds that the error patterns reflect the instructional program.

GOODMAN, KENNETH S. "Analysis of Oral Reading Miscues: Applied Psycholinguistics," *Reading Research Quarterly*, 5 (Fall 1969), 9-30.

Offers a theoretical argument that reading must be considered a psycholinguistic process. Author then presents a taxonomy for the depth analysis of oral reading miscues.

GOODMAN, KENNETH S. "A Linguistic Study of Cues and Miscues in Reading," *Elementary English*, 42 (October 1965), 639-643.

Analyzes miscues—the unexpected responses of readers. Finds that primary children could read many words in context which they could not read in lists. Concludes that the overwhelming reason for regressions (repetition) in reading was to correct prior errors.

GOODMAN, KENNETH S. (Ed.). *Miscue Analysis: Applications to Reading Instruction.* Urbana-Champaign, Illinois: Eric Clearinghouse on Reading and Communication Skills, October 1973.

Introduces the concepts behind miscue analysis as a window on the reading process and explores applications to the classroom.

GOODMAN, KENNETH S., and YETTA M. GOODMAN. "Learning about Psycholinguistic Processes by Analyzing Oral Reading," *Harvard Educational Review,* 47, 3 (1977), 317-333.

Discusses miscue analysis within a psycholinguistic view of reading as a language process. Shows how a typology of miscues serves to uncover the reader's depth structure processing abilities. Examines some implications of miscue analysis for research and teaching of reading.

GOODMAN, YETTA M. "Reading Diagnosis—Qualitative or Quantitative?" *Reading Teacher,* 26, 1 (October 1972), 32.

Suggests the use of miscue analysis for qualitative reading diagnosis. Reader is reminded that miscues are to be studied not just counted.

JONGSMA, KATHLEEN. "The Effect of Training in Miscue Analysis on Teacher's Perspectives of Oral Reading Behaviors," *Reading World,* 18, 1 (October 1978), 85-90.

Assesses the results of a teacher training program in miscue analysis in terms of teacher attitude toward oral reading. Results indicate that teachers become more aware of students' strengths and weaknesses after receiving training.

LAMBERG, WALTER J., and JOSEPH McCALEB. "Performance by Prospective Teachers in Distinguishing Dialect Feature and Miscues Unrelated to Dialect," *Journal of Reading,* 20, 7 (April 1977), 581-584.

Results show that reading students are not consistently identifying miscues with dialect features. These results cast doubt on the objectivity of informal reading inventories.

LUNDSTEEN, SARA W. "On Developmental Relations between Language Learning and Reading," *Elementary School Journal,* January 1977, 192-203.

Discusses the issue of errors in reading and suggests that some errors do not interfere with comprehension and that learning is facilitated if children are not worried about errors.

NURSS, J.R. "Oral Reading Errors and Reading Comprehension," *Reading Teacher*, 22 (March 1969), 523-527.

Examines reading errors by second grade children in relation to syntactic complexity in order to assess reading comprehension. Conclusions indicate that evaluation of types of reading errors can give insight into reading comprehension.

PAGE, WILLIAM D. *Concise Miscue Bibliography*. EDRS, 1973.

Provides a comprehensive bibliography on the methodology of miscue research and application of theory to practice.

RECHT, DONNA R. "The Self-Correction Process in Reading," *Reading Teacher*, 29, 7 (April 1976), 632-636.

Studies the use of self-correction in reading and concludes that it provides an indication of the reader's interaction with the text for meaning.

RUPLEY, WILLIAM H. "Miscue Analysis Research: Implications for Teacher and Researcher," *Reading Teacher*, 30, 5 (February 1977), 580-583.

Cites four studies focusing on miscue analysis and understanding the reading process and the application of miscue analysis to classroom reading instruction.

SCHLIEPER, ANNE. "Oral Reading Errors in Relation to Grade and Level of Skill," *Reading Teacher*, 31, 3 (December 1977), 283-287.

Studies the relationship of grade, miscues, and reading proficiency. Results show that, as the reading process matures, strategies are based more on meaning and syntax.

WEBER, ROSE-MARIE. "A Linguistic Analysis of First Grade Reading Errors," *Reading Research Quarterly*, 5 (Spring 1970), 427-451.

Analyzes reading errors according to level of sounds and letters, word structure, grammatical structure, and semantic consistency. Discusses the results of each level as well as their interrelationships. Concludes that the structure and meaning of language influence how children read and that children grow in their efficient use of letter-sound patterns. Describes the difference between faster and slower moving readers.

RELATIONSHIP BETWEEN ORAL AND WRITTEN LANGUAGE

Though a lot is being learned, there is still considerable disagreement on the relationship of oral language to written language and how these relationships affect development in each. One view is that written language is a representation of oral language; another is that they are parallel in literate societies and each represents meaning with the common language base underlying both.

ALLEN, HAROLD B. "Ambiguous Phonetics," *Elementary English*, 45 (May 1968), 600-601.

States that phonics asks the question, "What do these letters represent?" Phonetics is the scientific study of the sounds made by the human speech organs. Allen discusses each and the importance of distinguishing these terms.

ARTLEY, A. STERL. "Phonics Revisited," *Language Arts*, 54, 2 (February 1977), 121-126.

Reviews the literature on phonics and concludes that instruction in phonics should be minimized.

BAILEY, MILDRED H. "The Utility of Phonic Generalizations in Grades One through Six," *Reading Teacher*, 20 (February 1967), 413-418.

Redoes Clymer's study on phonic generalizations in primary grades to grades one to six using eight basals excluding single word occurrences, place names, proper names, and foreign words. With few exceptions, only five out of forty-five generalizations were simple to understand and apply to large numbers of words.

BERKO, JEAN. "The Child's Language and Written Language," *Education*, 85 (November 1965), 151-153.

Suggests that the closer the relationship is between the child's spoken language and the written language, the easier learning language related activities should be.

BOIARSKY, CAROLYN. "Consistency of Spelling and Pronunciation Deviations of Appalachian Students," *Modern Language Journal*, 53 (May 1969), 347-350.

Reports a study on the relationship between spelling and pronunciation of Applachian students. Boiarsky's conclusions suggest that Appalachian dialect is associated with spelling performance. Although reading is not discussed, there is information presented which may be of interest to some reading teachers.

CARTERETTE, EDWARD C., and MARGARET H. JONES. "Phoneme and Letter Patterns in Children's Language," in Kenneth S. Goodman (Ed.), *The Psycholinguistic Nature of the Reading Process*. Detroit: Wayne State University Press, 1968, 103-165.

Studies the sequential constraints on letters in a variety of written texts. Describes study of sequential constraints on phonemes in children's speech at the same grade levels.

DENBURG, SUSAN DALFEN. "The Interaction of Picture and Print in Reading Instruction: Abstracted Report," *Reading Research Quarterly*, 12, 2 (1976-1977), 176-188.

Reports support for the idea that improvement of word identification through context results from the use of information provided by accompanying pictorial or syntactic information.

DOWNING, JOHN. "Is Literacy Acquisition Easier in Some Languages Than in Others?" *Visible Language*, 7 (Spring 1973), 145-154.

Discusses the issues of differentness and degrees of difficulties for beginning readers which might result from different orthographies. Argues that the quantity of letters to be learned in a system is less a factor than the amount of repetition or redundancy in that system.

DOWNING, JOHN. "A Psycholinguistic Theory for i.t.a.," *Elementary English*, 47 (November 1970), 953-961.

Relates this orthographic innovation to psycholinguistic theory.

EAGAN, RUTH. "An Investigation into the Relationship of the Pausing Phenomena in Oral Reading and Reading Comprehension," *Alberta*

Journal of Educational Research, 21, 4 (December 1975), 278-288.

Studies the use of pauses in oral reading and seeks to determine if those pauses are observable features of the verbal processing system employed in oral and silent reading. Pauses are related to the subjects' comprehension abilities.

FRY, MAURINE A., and CAROLE SCHULTE JOHNSON. "Oral Language Production and Reading Achievement among Selected Students," *Journal of American Indian Education*, 13, 1 (October 1973), 22-27.

Studies the relation between reading achievement and oral language development using Pima-Maricopa Indian subjects from both public and Bureau of Indian Affairs day schools.

GILLOOLY, W.B. "The Influence of Writing-System Characteristics on Learning to Read," *Reading Research Quarterly*, 8, 2 (Winter 1973), 167-199.

Contains an analysis of English orthography and discusses some historical, cultural, and experimental influences on the behavioral effects of the writing system (reading).

GLAZER, SUSAN MANDEL, and LESLEY MANDEL MORROW. "The Syntactic Complexity of Primary Grade Children's Oral Language and Primary Grade Reading Materials: A Comparative Analysis," *Journal of Reading Behavior*, 10, 2 (Summer 1978), 200-201.

Compares the syntax of oral language of six, seven, and eight year olds with the syntax of the written language in instructional reading materials.

GLEITMAN, LILA R., and PAUL ROZIN. "Teaching Reading by Use of a Syllabary" (logographic writing system), *Reading Research Quarterly*, 8, 4 (Summer 1973) 447-483.

Shows that kindergarten children, both innercity and suburban, can easily acquire a twenty-three element syllabary. Views oral speech as the primary form of language and reading as a translation of written symbols into speech.

GLEITMAN, LILA R., and PAUL ROZIN. "Phoenician Go Home" (a response to Goodman), *Reading Research Quarterly*, 8, 4 (Summer 1974), 494-501.

Responds to K.S. Goodman's criticisms of the syllable approach, contending that this method is a natural use of the alphabetic principles of English writing.

GOODMAN, KENNETH S. "The 13th Easy Way to Make Learning to Read Difficult: A Reaction to Gleitman and Rozin," *Reading Research Quarterly*, 8, 4 (Summer 1973), 484-493.

Argues that while black children can learn Chinese characters, it cannot be concluded that a syllable approach to reading is justified. Suggests that a much broader base of psycholinguistic principles needs to be applied to reading methods and instructional materials.

GOODMAN, KENNETH S. "Decoding—From Code to What?" *Journal of Reading*, 14, 7 (April 1971), 455-463.

Challenges the use of the term "decoding" as a euphemism for phonics and argues that only when readers go from print to meaning can they be said to decode. Recoding is going from print to sound.

GRAHAM, RICHARD T., and E. HUGH RUDORF. "Dialect and Spelling," *Elementary English*, 47 (March 1970), 363-376.

Reports a study to discover whether sixth graders would exhibit significant differences in their spelling errors as related to phonetic differences in their dialects. Although not specifically related to reading, there is interesting data presented with suggestions for further research projects.

HALLE, MORRIS. "Some Thoughts on Spelling," in Kenneth S. Goodman and James T. Fleming (Eds.), *Psycholinguistics and the Teaching of Reading*. Newark, Delaware: International Reading Association, 1969, 17-24.

Presents Halle's argument that English orthography is not the hodgepodge that it is normally assumed to be but is, in fact, a good fit for English phonology.

HIGGINBOTTOM, ELEANOR M. "A Study of the Representation of English Vowel Phonemes in the Orthography," *Language and Speech*, 5 (1962), 67-117.

Reports a study which sought to correlate the phonemes of English speech with the graphemes of writing, as part of a program to make it possible for a machine to read graphemic sequences and derive spoken forms.

JOHNS, JERRY L. "Speaking, Listening, Writing," *Reading Teacher*, 29, 5 (February 1976), 458-459.

States arguments against teachers' expectations of perfection in reading performance.

KLEEDERMAN, FRANCES F. "Why Henry Made It: A Reply to S. Alan Cohen," *Reading World*, 17, 1 (October 1977), 1-6.

Examines relationships among language, cognitive strategies, and reading. Discusses the social and ethnic differences in the socialization of cognitive and communicative strategies among diverse groups.

KLEIMAN, GLENN M. "Speech Recoding in Reading," *Journal of Verbal Learning and Verbal Behavior*, 14, 4 (August 1975), 323-339.

Explores the idea of recoding to speech during reading and whether this phenomenon occurs prior to or after lexical access or not at all. Three experiments were conducted and a model was formulated in which lexical access precedes speech recoding.

LeFEVRE, CARL A. "The Trouble with Phonics: Some Constructive Suggestions," in M.S. Johnson and R.A. Kress (Eds.), *Thought-Language-Reading*, 1969 Annual Reading Institute. Philadelphia: Temple University, 1970, 47-56.

Presents sound linguistic information regarding phonetics, phonemics, and graphics after presenting some misconceptions teachers have regarding phonics. Lefevre also makes the case for differentiating spelling from reading and writing.

LEVY, BETTY ANN. "Speech Analysis During Sentence Processing: Reading and Listening," *Visible Language*, 12, 1 (Winter 1978), 81-99.

Presents evidence against the notion that speech recoding precedes lexical access. Discusses the possibility that recoding occurs in memory and word units are held in speech form until comprehension of larger discourse units (phrases, sentences) occurs.

LOTZ, JOHN. "Comment: The Role of Script in Describing the Languages of the World," *Visible Language*, 5, 1 (Winter 1971), 75-81.

Writes from the viewpoint that speech is the primary medium of language and examines some of the relationships between written and spoken languages which influence the script used in writing.

LUTZ, JOHN. "Some Comments about Psycholinguistic Research and Education," *Reading Teacher*, 28, 1 (October 1974), 36-39.

Differentiates between reading competence and reading performance and examines ten basal series in terms of language structure complexity, compares this complexity with children's potential, and hypothesizes that not until about fourth grade do books utilize more complex structures.

MATTINGLY, IGNATIUS G., and JAMES F. KAVANAGH. "The Relationships between Speech and Reading," *Linguistic Reporter*, 14, 5 (October 1972).

Argues that reading is a secondary language, not a primary linguistic activity. Suggests that reading is dependent on an awareness of morphophonemic segments, use of short term memory, and other aspects of listening and speaking.

OLSON, DAVID R. "From Utterance to Text: The Bias of Language in Speech and Writing," *Harvard Educational Review*, 47, 3 (August 1977), 257-281.

Compares conflicting conceptions of meaning in Chomsky's sense of ideation and the general written and spoken discourse sense of communication. Looks particularly at differences in terms of strictness and structure.

PAGE, WILLIAM D. "The Post Oral Reading Cloze Test: New Link between Oral Reading and Comprehension," *Journal of Reading Behavior*, 7, 4 (Winter 1975), 383-389.

Discusses the relationship of comprehension as measured by cloze and oral reading responses.

READ, CHARLES. *Children's Categorization of Speech Sounds*. Urbana-Champaign, Illinois: National Council of Teachers of English, 1975.

Categorizes speech sounds produced by preschoolers and concludes that beginning spelling is naturally based on an intuitive knowledge of English phonology.

SCHALLERT, DIANE L., GLENN M. KLEIMAN, and ANN D. RUBIN. *Analysis of Differences between Written and Oral Language*, Technical Report No. 29. Urbana-Champaign, Illinois: University of Illinois, Center for the Study of Reading, April 1977.

Proposes that differences in oral and written language produce differences in the knowledge and skills necessary for comprehension of these two forms of language.

SMILEY, SANDRA S., and others. *Recall of Thematically Relevant Material by Adolescent Good and Poor Readers as a Function of Written versus Oral Presentation*, Technical Report No. 23. Urbana-Champaign, Illinois: University of Illinois, Center for the Study of Reading, March 1977.

Examines subjects' comprehension in reading and listening situations. Finds a general deficit in comprehension among poor readers regardless of the method of presentation. Hypothesizes that reading and listening involve a similar comprehension process.

SMITH, FRANK. "Phonology and Orthography: Reading and Writing," *Elementary English*, 49, 7 (November 1972), 1075-1088.

Considers two methods whereby words are identified: 1) immediate word identification (relying primarily on visual features), and 2) mediated word identification (use of context to associate the word with meaning). Concludes that the relationship between orthography and phonology is used infrequently in the identification of words.

STRICKLAND, RUTH G. "The Language of Elementary School Children: Its Relationship to the Language of Reading Textbooks and the Quality of Reading of Selected Children," *Bulletin of School of Education* (Indiana University), 38 (July 1962).

Contains a series of related studies that uses linguistic description of the structure of children's language and compares it to the structure of the language in their reading books. It is generally the same analysis used by Loban. The study supports the contention of many linguists that children come to school with a fairly complete mastery of the structure of English.

VENEZKY, RICHARD L. "English Orthography: Its Graphical Structure and Its Relation to Sound," *Reading Research Quarterly*, 2 (Spring 1967), 75-105.

Suggests that the translation of written symbols to sound is the only language skill unique to reading, questions some sacred cows in reading, and offers alternate factors. Summarizes patterns of the 20,000 most common words in English for translating from spelling to sound.

WARDHAUGH, RONALD. "A Linguist Looks at Phonics," *Elementary English*, 48 (January 1971), 61-66.

Examines certain understandings about linguistics necessary to those involved in reading instruction. Wardhaugh attempts to dispel many misconceptions teachers have about phonetics as well as phonics instruction.

WEAVER, WENDELL W., and ALBERT J. KINGSTON. "Modeling the Effects of Oral Language upon Reading Language," *Reading Research Quarterly*, 8, 4 (Summer 1972), 613-627.

Studies the manner in which information is used by an individual, i.e. "sign behavior." Formulates a model of reading which incorporates knowledge about this processing of information.

WEIGL, E. "Neuropsychological Approach to the Problem of Transcoding," *Linguistics*, 154/155 (June 15, 1975), 105-136.

Deals with the process of transcoding; i.e., switching from one sign system to another, such as spoken speech and written speech or numerical words and numerical figures. Hypothesizes that the different systems must be related by corresponding structures.

WILKINSON, ANDREW. "Oracy and Reading," *Elementary English*, 51, 8 (November-December 1974), 1102-1109.

Examines research on oracy and reading, language acquisition and reading, features of spoken and written language, and reading and prior linguistic knowledge.

WOOD, KARLYN E. "A Comparison of Characteristics of Dictated Language of First Grade Children with Oral Language and Performance in Reading," *Child Study Journal*, 8, 1 (1978), 55-63.

Compares first grade children's oral language, dictated language, and reading performance.

THE READING TEACHER AND LINGUISTICS

In this section, we include articles which focus on the linguistic knowledge needed by teachers of reading. Articles dealing with preservice and inservice teacher education are also included.

ANGELOTTI, MICHAEL. "Psycholinguistics and the Reading/Language Arts Teacher: A Time for Learning," *English Education*, 9, 1 (Fall 1977), 31-42.

Presents approaches and objectives for an inservice program or a college course in psycholinguistics and reading.

BOTEL, MORTON. "What Linguistics Says to This Teacher of Reading and Spelling," *Reading Teacher*, 18 (December 1964), 188-193.

Discusses intonation and patterns in spelling and syntax. Botel suggests ways children can be helped to develop and use linguistic abilities in reading.

COOPER, BERNICE. "Contributions of Linguistics in Teaching Reading," *Education*, 85 (May 1965), 529-532.

States that at present the greatest contribution of linguistics to the teaching of reading may be to give the teacher greater understanding of the nature of language. The author believes that current suggestions by linguists for beginning reading instruction may then be oversimplified. She uses Fries to demonstrate her position.

FILLION, BRYANT, FRANK SMITH, and MERRILL SWAIN. "Language 'Basics' for Language Teachers: Toward a Set of Universal Considerations," *Language Arts*, 53, 7 (October 1976), 740-745, 757.

Presents information about language that is considered necessary for language teachers.

FORESTER, ANNE D. "What Teachers Can Learn from 'Natural Readers'," *Reading Teacher*, 31, 2 (November 1977), 160-166.

Asks teachers to observe those children who begin to read naturally by themselves. Suggests that important insights into the reading process may be gained by such observation.

GOODMAN, YETTA M. "Using Children's Miscues for Teaching Reading Strategies," *Reading Teacher*, 24 (February 1970), 455-459.

States that some reading miscues are better than others. They reveal children's strengths as well as weaknesses. Teachers need to know which are good miscues that indicate the reader's control of the reading process.

GOODMAN, YETTA M., and CAROLYN BURKE. "Do They Read What They Speak?" *Grade Teacher*, 26 (March 1969), 144-150.

Indicates how linguistic principles can be applied to analysis of reading miscues and what insights this can give a teacher concerning the strengths and weaknesses of a specific reader.

GOVE, MARY K. "Psycholinguistics and the Reading Teacher," *Language Arts*, 53 (March 1976), 326-328.

Emphasizes that words and sound-symbol associations should not be presented out of context but, rather, strategies need to be developed using sense of the sentence, graphic cues, and other meaning cues.

HALL, MARYANNE, and CHRISTOPHER J. RAMIG. *Linguistic Foundations for Reading*. Columbus, Ohio: Charles E. Merrill, 1978.

Presents pertinent linguistic information written especially for teachers.

HARSTE, JEROME C. "Understanding the Hypothesis, It's the Teacher that Makes the Difference: Part I," *Reading Horizons*, 18, 1 (Fall 1977), 32-43. Part II, 18, 2 (Winter 1978), 89-98.

Examines teachers' theoretical models of the reading process and describes the consistency of classroom application based on these models. Offers suggestions for teachers to strengthen their theoretical positions.

HODGES, RICHARD E., and E HUGH RUDORF. *Language and Learning to Read: What Teachers Should Know about Language*. New York: Houghton Mifflin, 1972.

Presents a collection of papers for teachers concerning the areas of language and reading.

KOPFSTEIN, ROBERT W. "Fluent Reading, Language, and the Reading Teacher," *Reading Teacher*, 32, 2, 195-197.

Emphasizes teachers' responsibilities in understanding the reading process and its relationship to linguistic development. Focuses on perception, semantic and syntactic cues, and strategies for comprehension.

MALMSTROM, JEAN. *Understanding Language: A Primer for the Language Arts Teacher.* New York: St. Martin's Press, 1977.

Discusses the comprehensiveness of language arts instruction and includes some practical programs for teachers. Discusses reading from a psycholinguistic perspective.

MARTIN, BILL, JR. "Helping Children Claim Language through Literature," *Elementary English*, 45 (May 1968), 583-591.

Makes distinctions among the language of the home, society, and literature. Martin proposes use of the language of literature to bridge the gap between "home" and "societal" language, which he feels will build a love of language in children.

McCULLOUGH, CONSTANCE M. "Linguistics, Psychology, and the Teaching of Reading," *Elementary English*, 44 (April 1967), 353-362.

Raises the importance of teachers being sophisticated about language and examines the decoding of meanings.

SHAFER, ROBERT E. "What Teachers Should Know about Children's Language," *Elementary English*, 51, 4 (April 1974), 498-501.

Emphasizes that reading instruction should be based on knowledge about children's language. Presents new linguistic knowledge which is not compatible with certain reading instruction systems.

SHAFER, ROBERT E. "What Teachers Should Know about Psycholinguistics in Reading and Miscue Analysis," *English Quarterly*, 10, 1 (Spring 1977), 49-54.

Examines the work of psycholinguists dealing with applications to the classroom and teacher education programs.

SHREWSBURY, JAMES B., JR. "Linguistics and the Elementary Teacher: A Call for a Change in Certification Requirements," *Elementary English*, 46 (March 1969), 342-346.

Explores the state of course requirements in linguistics for teacher certification. Author proposes a linguistic course for teachers.

TOVEY, DUANE R. "A Psycholinguistic Analysis of Reading Activities," *Reading World*, 17, 2 (December 1977), 125-134.

Proposes that until classroom teachers become cognizant of the reading process, the learning process, and the functioning of language, reading instruction will continue to concentrate heavily on the visual elements.

SYNTAX, GRAMMAR, AND INTONATION

These selections feature concern for how language structure is involved in reading. Developments in applications parallel a shift of concern in theoretical linguistics from syntax to semantic and pragmatics. Recent work by psychologists on text analysis has dealt only minimally with syntactic aspects, usually drawing on case grammar. Dates on articles in this section reflect the sparseness of publications in recent years.

ALLEN, ROBERT L. "Better Reading through the Recognition of Grammatical Relations," *Reading Teacher*, 18 (December 1964), 194-198.

Presents Allen's argument that an analytical system he has devised—sector analysis—may be an effective method to teach children sentence analysis and make them better readers. Sector analysis emphasizes positions in constructions.

COWAN, J. RONAYNE. "Reading, Perceptual Strategies, and Contrastive Analysis," *Language Learning*, 26, 1 (June 1976), 95-109.

Provides a contrastive syntactic analysis using cross-cultural groups and languages. Discusses results in terms of the process of reading and applicability of second language learning models.

DAVIS, O.L., and JOAN G. SEIFERT. "Some Linguistic Features of Five Literature Books for Children," *Elementary English*, 44 (December 1967), 878-882.

Reports a study designed to reveal language features used in five books for children. The authors analyzed communicative units, structural patterns, movables, and subordinating structures.

EMIG, JANET A. "Grammar and Reading," in H. Alan Robinson (Ed.), *Recent Developments in Reading*. Chicago: University of Chicago Press, 1965, 125-129.

Discusses the intuitive knowledge children have of grammar, phonology, morphology, and syntax. Emig suggests building reading skills on this intuitive knowledge.

HERRIOT, PETER. "Comprehension of Syntax," *Child Development*, 39 (March 1968), 273-282.

Presents a study which was conducted to see how English children match active and passive sense and nonsense sentences to pictures. Author concludes that syntax of a sentence has semantic reference and that sentence form is more difficult for children to comprehend than form classes.

HUNT, KELLOGG W. "Recent Measures in Syntactic Development," *Elementary English*, 43 (November 1966), 732-739.

Reports that the length of the clause, rather than the sentence, is the best indicator of maturity in writing. Similarly, Hunt demonstrates that materials are difficult to comprehend in proportion to the lengths of clauses, not of sentences.

KAISER, ROBERT A., CHERYL F. NEILS, and BERNARD P. FLORIANI. "Syntactic Complexity of Primary Grade Reading Materials: A Preliminary Look," *Reading Teacher*, 29, 3 (December 1975), 262-266.

Studies some commonly used primary reading materials in terms of syntactic complexity.

LeFEVRE, CARL A. "Reading: Intonation and Punctuation," *Education*, 87 (May 1967), 525-530.

States that reading is greatly enhanced by the awareness of intonational features of English. Lefevre presents aspects of intonation including stress-timed rhythm, voice terminals and associated pauses, and punctuation to facilitate instruction.

LESGOLD, ALAN M. "Variability in Children's Comprehension of Syntactic Structures," *Journal of Educational Psychology*, 66, 3 (June 1974), 333-338.

Challenges Bormouth's difficulty ordering for anaphoric syntax. Believes that the evaluation used to determine ordering is invalid because of uncontrolled variability in semantic factors.

LLOYD, DONALD. "Intonation and Reading," *Education*, 85 (May 1964), 538-541.

States that knowledge from linguistic research related to intonation may be more useful to teachers of reading than the system of sound relationships. Reading should be related to the spoken language of the reader and intonation is an important aspect of this.

NEUWIRTH, SHARYN E. "A Look at Intersentence Grammar," *Reading Teacher*, 30, 1 (October 1976), 28-32.

Examines reading in a range beyond the sentence and suggests that there is information available at these levels that needs to be studied by psycholinguists.

NILAGUPTA, SIRIRAT. "The Relationship of Syntax to Readability for ESL Students in Thailand," *Journal of Reading*, 20, 7 (April 1977), 585-594.

Looks at Thai students who have studied English as a second language. Investigates the effects of syntax on their reading comprehension.

OHAUER, A. "A Comparison Study of Semantic and Syntactic Cueing by Low Reading Performance College Freshmen," in Frank Greene (Ed.), *Investigations Relating to Mature Reading*, Twenty-First Yearbook of the National Reading Conference, 1972.

Investigates the syntactic and semantic cueing systems in oral reading by studying the errors of low reading achieving college freshmen. Results are interpreted as support for the position that reading must involve comprehension at some level.

OTTO, JEAN. "Reading Cue Utilization by Low Achieving College Freshmen," *Journal of Reading Behavior*, 14, 1 (Spring 1977), 71-84.

Compares the use of graphic cues with syntactic and semantic processes for low achieving college freshmen.

PAGE, W.D., and K.L. CARLSON. "The Process of Observing Oral Reading Scores," *Reading Horizons*, 15, 3 (1975), 147-150.

Discusses the methods used by qualified reading specialists in the grading, interpretation, and use of oral reading evaluations.

PIVAL, JEAN G. "Stress, Pitch, and Structure: Tools in the Diagnosis and Treatment of Reading Ills," *Elementary English*, 45 (April 1968), 458-463, 467.

States that oral reading can provide insights into a reader's inability to use intonation characteristics properly. According to the author, the reader needs to be aware of intonation patterns. Stress, pitch, and structure are defined and suggestions for instruction are presented.

REDDIN, ESTOY. "Research: Syntactical Structure and Reading Comprehension," *Reading Teacher*, 23 (February 1970), 467-469.

Reviews studies which have dealt with the relationship of the syntactical structure of written material and the awareness of those structures in potential readers.

RICHEK, MARGARET ANN. "Effect of Sentence Complexity on the Reading Comprehension of Syntactic Structures," *Journal of Educational Psychology*, 68, 6 (December 1976), 800-806.

Studies and analyzes the effects of sentence complexity on the comprehension of syntactic structures within the sentence.

SILER, EARL. "The Effects of Syntactic and Semantic Constraints on the Oral Reading Performance of Second and Fourth Graders," *Reading Research Quarterly*, 9, 4 (1973-1974), 583-602.

Looks at oral reading performance in terms of the effects of syntax and/or semantic violations. Variance of syntax appears to exercise a greater influence than semantics.

SMITH, WILLIAM L. "The Controlled Instrument Procedure for Studying the Effect of Syntactic Sophistication on Reading: A Second Study," *Journal of Reading Behavior*, 5, 4 (Fall 1973).

Presents the results of an experimental situation relating the reader's syntactical sophistication and the material being read.

SMITH, WILLIAM L., and GEORGE E. MASON. "Syntactic Control in Writing: Better Comprehension," *Reading Teacher*, 15 (1972), 355-358.

Compares the relationship of the syntax of reading materials to that of the child and suggests that one way to increase comprehension is to match syntax, not simplify it.

STOODT, BARBARA D. "The Relationship between Understanding Grammatical Conjunctions and Reading Comprehension," *Elementary English*, 49 (April 1972), 502-504.

Explores a subject's understanding of conjunctions and his reading comprehension. Looks at various levels of difficulty of conjunctions as well as the variables of socioeconomic status, sex, and intelligence.

TATHAM, SUSAN MASLAND. "Reading Comprehension of Materials Written with Select Oral Language Patterns: A Study at Grades Two and Four," *Reading Research Quarterly*, 5 (Spring 1970), 402-426.

Reports using a comprehension measure based on children matching a sentence to a matching picture. Tatham concludes that her subjects are better at comprehending materials written in language patterns more familiar to them (based on Strickland's analysis) than those written in less familiar patterns. Additional information is provided on grade level difference and implications for reading instruction, and materials are suggested.

TYLER, PRISCILLA. "Sound Patterns and Sense," *Education*, 84 (May 1963).

Discusses the relationship of stress, pitch, and juncture to listening and reading comprehension.

WISHER, ROBERT A. "The Effects of Syntactic Expectations During Reading," *Journal of Educational Psychology*, 68, 5 (October 1976), 597-602.

Finds that the time required for reading decreases if the subject is aware of the sentence's syntactic structure before reading. Explains those results in terms of reading being an interactive process involving linguistic decisions and memory storage.

WOLFRAM, WALT. "Extended Notions of Grammar and Reading Comprehension," *Journal of Reading Behavior*, 8, 3 (Fall 1976), 247-258.

States that to comprehend the relationship between comprehension and grammar, the boundaries of traditional syntax must be expanded to include language usage in the real world.

ZEMAN, S.S. "Reading Comprehension and Writing of Second and Third Graders," *Reading Teacher*, 23 (November 1969), 144-150.

Investigates the relationship between reading comprehension with basic sentence types and the sentence patterns used in the written compositions of second and third graders. In some sentence types, the grade was more significant than any other variable. Children use three structural patterns with similar frequency regardless of reading comprehension scores.

TESTING AND EVALUATION

A literature has been developing in recent years that critiques common testing practices and offers alternatives based on linguistic and psycholinguistic perspectives. These selections represent that literature.

BORTNICK, ROBERT, and GENEVIEVE S. LOPARDO. "The Cloze Procedure: A Multipurpose Classroom Tool," *Reading Improvement*, 13, 2 (Summer 1976), 113-117.

Introduces the cloze procedure to the classroom teachers as being appropriate for instruction, diagnosis, measurement, and evaluation.

DAVIES, PETER. "Language Skills in Sentence Level Reading Tests," *Reading*, 11, 1 (April 1977), 27-35.

Recommends the use of sentence completion tasks under certain conditions for reading assessment and for evaluation of language development and understanding of syntactic structures.

FARR, ROGER. "Is Johnny's/Mary's Reading Getting Worse?" *Educational Leadership*, 34, 7 (April 1977), 521-527.

Discusses the current federal program emphasis on basic skills and drill exercises and suggests that this may be related to a decline in inferential reading scores.

GEISSAL, MARY ANN, and JUNE D. KNAFLE. "A Linguistic View of Auditory Discrimination Tests and Exercises," *Reading Teacher*, 31, 2 (November 1977), 134-144.

Questions the relationship of abilities as measured by auditory discrimination tests and reading ability.

GOODMAN, KENNETH S. "Do You Have to Be Smart to Read? Do You Have to Read to Be Smart?" *Reading Teacher*, 28, 7 (April 1975), 625-632.

Discusses the circular maze of testing and teaching and the problems that result when children do not fall within the predicted pattern. Proposes that meaningful communication is the purpose of reading—not mastery of subskills.

GOODMAN, KENNETH S. "Effective Teachers of Reading Know Language and Children," *Elementary English*, 51, 6 (September 1974), 823-828.

Argues against the concept of sequential skill development as being indefensible and suggests that current reading tests are reinforcing misconceptions about the reading process.

GOODMAN, KENNETH S. "Testing in Reading: A General Critique," in Robert Ruddell (Ed.), *Accountability and Reading Instruction*. Urbana-Champaign, Illinois: National Council of Teachers of English, 1973, 21-33.

Examines normed and criterion referenced tests regarding uses and issues in utilization, interpretation, question design, function of scores, reading theory, and accountability.

GOODMAN, YETTA M. "Kid Watching: An Alternative to Testing," *National Elementary Principal*, 57, 4 (June 1978), 41-45.

Argues against standardized testing as providing very limited information. Suggests that successful teachers have traditionally looked at the whole child to determine the reasons behind the child's responses.

JOHNSON, DALE D., and P. DAVID PEARSON. "Skills Management: A Critique," *Reading Teacher*, 19, 3 (May 1975), 757-764.

Discusses the skills management criterion referenced systems as inappropriate since no basis for the separation, sequencing, or even the skills themselves can be found to be related to reading achievement.

PAGE, WILLIAM D. "Comprehending and Cloze Performance," *Reading World*, 17, 1 (October 1977), 17-21.

Presents results from a comparison study of oral reading comprehending scores and post oral reading cloze test scores.

SMITH, LAURA, and CONSTANCE WEAVER. "A Psycholinguistic Look at the Informal Reading Inventory, Part I: Looking at the Quality of Readers' Miscues—A Rationale and an Easy Method," *Reading Horizons*, 19, 1 (Fall 1978).

Looks at the informal reading inventory from a psycholinguistic perspective. Suggests a method for looking at the quality of the errors in the IRI.

THEORIES OF READING

The work on theories of reading continues to grow. Most of it draws on linguistics and psycholinguistics. Some have attempted general theories of the reading process; some have confined themselves to "microtheories" of aspects of reading. Some attempts have been made at theories of reading instruction and reading development. We include all of those here.

ATHEY, IRENE J. "Language Models and Reading," *Reading Research Quarterly*, 7, 1 (1971), 16-110.

Summarizes models of language and reading. Suggests needed research.

CALFEE, ROBERT C., and PRISCILLA A. DRUM. "Learning to Read: Theory, Research, and Practice," *Curriculum Inquiry*, 8, 3 (Fall 1978).

Focuses on the formulation of an "independent process model for early reading." Discusses historical influences; theoretical approaches of organization and integration; research; differences in individual achievement, curriculum, and teaching practices; projections for the future.

CAMBOURNE, BRIAN. "Getting to Goodman: An Analysis of the Goodman Model of Reading with Some Suggestions for Evaluation," *Reading Research Quarterly*, 12, 4 (1976-1977), 605-636.

Relates the Goodman model of reading to current psycholinguistic research. Offers criteria for evaluation of the model.

CARROLL, JOHN B. "The Analysis of Reading Instruction: Perspectives from Psychology and Linguistics," *Theories of Learning and Instruction*, National Society for the Study of Education, Sixty-Third Yearbook, Part I, 1964, 335-353.

Presents the application of psychological theory and linguistic knowledge to the teaching of reading. Deals more with the sound-symbol relationship, word recognition, and stimulus-response relationships of reading behavior than with the areas of syntactic and semantic relationships of utterances. Suggests numerous problems of psychological theory in describing reading behavior.

GEYER, JOHN J. "Comprehensive and Partial Models Related to the Reading Process," *Reading Research Quarterly*, 7, 4 (Summer 1972), 541-587.

Summarizes some of the literature on information processing reading models. Contends that the information processing point of view can serve to facilitate communication among the various fields studying and contributing to our knowledge about reading.

GOODMAN, KENNETH S. "Psycholinguistic Universals in the Reading Process," *Journal of Typographic Research*, 4 (Spring 1970), 103-110.

Expands on a psycholinguistic theory of the reading process to include languages and orthographies other than English. Speculates on the extent to which reading is a universal process.

GOODMAN, KENNETH S. "Reading: A Psycholinguistic Guessing Game," in Harry Singer and Robert Ruddell (Eds.), *Theoretical Models and Processes in Reading*. Newark, Delaware: International Reading Association, 1970, 259-272.

Describes the reading process as a guessing game in which the reader samples from the text using minimal graphic, semantic, and syntactic information to predict the meaning. A model of the process is included.

GOUGH, PHILIP B. "One Second of Reading," *Visible Language*, 6, 4 (Autumn 1972), 291-320.

Views one second of reading and the events that occur during that brief period. The succession of occurrences includes the formation of visual icons, letter identification, and transpositions into abstract phonemic representations leading to meaning.

HOCHBERG, JULIAN, and VIRGINIA BROOKS. "Reading as an Intentional Behavior," in Harry Singer and Robert Ruddell (Eds.), *Theoretical Models and Processes in Reading*. Newark, Delaware: International Reading Association, 1970, 304-315.

Asserts that readers use their knowledge "about language and about writers" even in deciding the points at which to make fixations. Authors feel intention is a vital part of initiating and maintaining reading behavior. Helping children to organize their intentions may involve encouraging children to predict and anticipate.

JENKINSON, MARION D. "Sources of Knowledge for Theories of Reading," *Journal of Reading Behavior*, 1 (Winter 1969), 11-29.

Discusses reasons for failure to evolve reading theories despite years of investigation. Jenkinson suggests the hope for model making in reading;

lists questions regarding the acquisition and assimilation of reading; and examines aspects of philosophy, linguistics, and psychology which might facilitate development of a learning theory.

KOLERS, PAUL A. "Reading Is Only Incidentally Visual," in Kenneth S. Goodman and James T. Fleming (Eds.), *Psycholinguistics and the Teaching of Reading*. Newark, Delaware: International Reading Association, 1969, 8-16.

Reviews Kolers' research on adult reading of distorted material. This material is either produced by geometrically transforming the letters or mixing languages for bilingual subjects. From a study of the errors subjects produce, author concludes that reading is only incidentally visual and therefore reading instruction should emphasize the "clue search and information-extracting characteristics of reading."

La BERGE, DAVID, and S. JAY SAMUELS. "Toward a Theory of Automatic Information Processing and Reading," *Cognitive Psychology*, 6, 2 (1974), 293-323.

Presents a model of information processing based on the identification of words from an analysis of visual features. Once the visual aspects have been identified, processing becomes automatic.

LeFEVRE, CARL A. "A Symposium on Reading Theory," *Journal of Reading Behavior*, 1 (Winter 1969), 3-9.

Concerns the multidisciplinary nature of reading content, process, and instruction, and the need for a theoretical framework for reading.

LLOYD, DONALD. "Reading American English as a Native Language," in J. Allen Figurel (Ed.), *Challenge and Experiment in Reading*, Proceedings of the International Reading Association, 7, 1962. New York: Scholastic Magazines, 247-251.

Demonstrates, with examples, how the reader puts his knowledge of language to work in reading. Discusses intonation, syntax, and vocabulary.

LLOYD, DONALD, and HARRY WARFEL. "The Structural Approach to Reading," *School and Society*, 85 (June 1957), 199-201.

Suggests that the key for learning to read lies in having children relate their own expert knowledge of oral language to the material they read. Presents linguistic principles about the relationship between speaking and writing.

MASSARO, DOMINIC W. "A Stage Model of Reading and Listening," *Visible Language*, 12, 1 (Winter 1978), 3-23.

Incorporates both reading and listening in a four stage language processing model including: feature detection, primary and secondary recognitions, recording, and rehearsal.

PEARSON, P. DAVID. "A Psycholinguistic Model of Reading," *Language Arts*, 53, 3 (March 1976), 309-314.

Gives a brief review of language models of Smith, Goodman, and Samuels, and concentrates on areas relating to pedagogy: categorization and evaluation of instructional activities, analysis of reading disabilities, and examination of oral reading errors. Concludes that some current practices in reading instruction are in error.

ROSENBLATT, LOUISE M. *The Reader, the Text, the Poem*. Carbondale, Illinois: Southern Illinois University Press, 1978.

Presents Rosenblatt's theory of transactional reading of the literary work. Focuses on the creative role of the reader as well as the significance of the text.

ROSENBLATT, LOUISE M. "Toward a Transactional Theory of Reading," *Journal of Reading Behavior*, 1 (Winter 1969), 31-50.

Presents a transactional view of reading which suggests the importance of the reader and text in a dynamic reading transaction. Rosenblatt raises research questions which need to be answered based on such a theory.

RUDDELL, ROBERT B. "Language Acquisition and the Reading Process," in Harry Singer and Robert Ruddell (Eds.), *Theoretical Models and Processes in Reading*. Newark, Delaware: International Reading Association, 1970, 1-19.

Summarizes research on child language development and relates it to reading and learning to read. Includes research recommendations and an extensive bibliography.

RUDDELL, ROBERT B. "Psycholinguistic Implications for a Systems of Communication Model," in Kenneth S. Goodman and James T. Fleming (Eds.), *Psycholinguistics and the Teaching of Reading*. Newark, Delaware: International Reading Association, 1969, 61-78.

Presents "...an overview of selected linguistic and psycholinguistic variables related to decoding and comprehending language." Ruddell then attempts to integrate these variables into a "system of communication model."

RYAN, ELLEN B., and MELVIN I. SEMMEL. "Reading as a Constructive Language Process," *Reading Research Quarterly*, 5 (Fall 1969), 59-83.

Views correspondences between printed and spoken messages as based more on meaning than on pairing visual and auditory forms. Authors assert that children should, therefore, be encouraged to develop strategies for getting meaning even in early instruction in reading.

SINGER, HARRY, and ROBERT B. RUDDELL (Eds.). *Theoretical Models and Processes of Reading*. Newark, Delaware: International Reading Association, 1970.

Part 1 contains original papers, some of which are cited separately in this bibliography under appropriate headings. Part 2 consists primarily of articles reprinted from other sources, several of which are cited in this bibliography from the original source.

SMITH, FRANK. *Psycholinguistics and Reading*. New York: Holt, Rinehart and Winston, 1973.

Discusses the applications of psycholinguistics for teachers and suggests its value for increasing knowledge about the process of reading.

SMITH, FRANK, and DEBORAH L. HOLMES. "The Independence of Letter, Word, and Meaning Identification in Reading," *Reading Research Quarterly*, 6 (Spring 1971), 394-415.

Distills from psychological, linguistic, and psycholinguistic research proof for the proposition that "Memory and visual information-processing constraints preclude the prior identification of individual letters or words if comprehension is to be achieved." Argues that the same text may be analyzed for letters, for words, or for meaning. Reading must involve the latter to be effective.

VENEZKY, RICHARD L., and ROBERT C. CALFEE. "The Reading Competency Model," in Harry Singer and Robert Ruddell (Eds.), *Theoretical Models and Processes of Reading*. Newark, Delaware: International Reading Association, 1970, 273-291.

Offers a model of competent reading consistent with structural linguistics and behavioral learning theory. Suggests programs of research for verifying the aspects of the model.

WEAVER, WENDELL W. "The Contribution of Research to Reading Theory," *Journal of Reading Behavior*, 1 (Spring 1969), 3-18.

Argues for theory in reading which can accommodate research findings and delineate needed research. Rejects several linguistic and psychological theoretical positions including nontheory.

WILLIAMS, JOANNA P. "Learning to Read: A Review of Theories and Models," *Reading Research Quarterly*, 8, 2 (Winter 1973), 121-146.

Reviews and discusses various reading theories and models.

WITTROCK, M.C., CAROLYN MARKS, and MARLEEN DOCTOROW. "Reading as a Generative Process," *Journal of Educational Psychology*, 67 (August 1975), 484-489.

States that phonetic, syntactic, and semantic processes are involved in reading and that meaning is generated through the application to the text of memory in terms of events and relations.

WORDS

"In the beginning was the word...." That's true as a preoccupation in looking at language and reading. But modern linguistic scholarship has caused the significance of "the word" as a language unit to be revalued. This section includes articles which have dealt with the word as a linguistic unit in reading.

ALLINGTON, RICHARD L. "The Visual Confusability of High Frequency Words," *Journal of Learning Disabilities*, 10, 7 (August-September 1977), 444-449.

Considers the problems of visual identification of first grade high frequency words. Presents evidence that words in isolation are difficult to identify and suggests that the word should be embedded in a meaningful unit.

CLEARY, DONNA McKEE. "Reading without Vowels: Some Implications," *Journal of Reading*, 20, 1 (October 1976), 52-56.

Illustrates the use of context clues by high school students to gain meaning from text.

DUNN-RANKIN, PETER. "Using After Images in the Analysis of Letter and Word Focalization," *Journal of Reading Behavior*, 9, 2 (Summer 1977), 113-122.

Investigates subjects' visual focal points when viewing letters, words, and phrases. Develops a model of visual preprocessing as related to reading which includes a subconscious control mechanism.

FINN, PATRICK J. "Word Frequency, Information Theory, and Cloze Performance: A Transfer Feature Theory of Processing in Reading," *Reading Research Quarterly*, 13, 4 (1977-1978), 508-537.

Presents an information theory which is a function of the quantity of lexical markers associated with the word and the number of markers supplied for the word through transfer features. The applications of this theory to identify high and low information words are discussed and the theory's consistency with three current reading models is examined.

GOODMAN, KENNETH S. "Influences of the Visual Peripheral Field in Reading," *Research in the Teaching of English*, 9, 2 (Fall 1975), 210-222.

Discusses the visual peripheral field and its relation to reading cues. Concludes that the influence of cues in this field is not random.

GOVE, PHILLIP B. "Reading from the Lexicographer's Viewpoint," *Reading Teacher*, 18 (December 1964), 199-201.

Discusses how lexicographers determine word meanings.

JOHNSON, NEAL F. "On the Function of Letters in Word Identification: Some Data and a Preliminary Model," *Journal of Verbal Learning and Verbal Behavior*, 14, 1 (1975), 17-29.

Provides a model of word perception based on the theory that a word is processed as a single unit and individual letters are not identified. Three experiments are reported.

JOHNSTON, JAMES C. "A Test of the Sophisticated Guessing Theory of Word Perception," *Cognitive Psychology*, 10, 2 (April 1978), 123-153.

Discusses word and letter perception. Finds that, if viewing conditions are difficult, a letter is identified more accurately in a common word than if the letter either stands alone or appears in a group of random letters.

LAZERSON, BARBARA HUNT. "The Influence of Highly Variable Spelling upon the Reading Performance of Skilled Readers of Modern English," *Reading Research Quarterly*, 10, 4 (1974-1975), 583-615.

Brings support to the theory that reading is a cognitive process. States that orthographic and syntactic-semantic information are stored in the brain and used during the reading process.

LeFEVRE, CARL A. "Simplistic Standard Word Perception Theory of Reading," *Elementary English*, 45 (March 1968), 349-353, 355.

Attacks the notion that the word is the unit in reading material. The author uses a psycholinguistic argument to support his view that the sentence is the basic meaning bearing unit in reading.

McCONAUGHY, STEPHANIE H. "Word Recognition and Word Meaning in the Total Reading Process," *Language Arts*, 55, 8 (November-December 1978), 946-956.

Provides a look at reading instruction from the perspective of the importance of meaning. Contains a comprehensive bibliography.

MELTZER, NANCY, and ROBERT HERSE. "The Boundaries of Written Words as Seen by First Graders," *Journal of Reading Behavior*, 1 (Summer 1969), 3-14.

Reports doubt that first graders really know what words are. The authors conducted a study in which they found that children frequently equate words and letters and go through a number of other misconceptions before becoming aware that space separates words.

MORRIS, PETER E. "Frequency and Imagery in Word Recognition: Further Evidence for an Attribute Model," *British Journal of Psychology*, Volume 59, Part I (February 1978), 69-75.

Incorporates a theory of word recognition with the system of memory processing. Suggests a model of decoding based on the memory marking and storing certain features which define a particular word.

NILES, JEROME A. "The Use of Featural and Letter Dependency Information in Word Recognition by Elementary School Children" (Abstract), *Reading Research Quarterly*, 11, 2 (1975-1976), 198-202.

Discusses Frank Smith's theory of sequential redundancy in terms of components, sequential dependency, and visual processing. Finds that some grade one subjects are naturally acquiring the abilities to process written text and that the use and development of sequential redundancy cannot be taught directly.

SHUY, ROGER W. "Some Language and Cultural Differences in a Theory of Reading," in Kenneth S. Goodman and James T. Fleming (Eds.), *Psycholinguistics and the Teaching of Reading*. Newark, Delaware: International Reading Association, 1969, 34-47.

Selects two dimensions of children's learning to read to illustrate the need for concern for how language is learned and how culture influences learning. Specifically, Shuy deals with dialect differences of black children and with syllables in English words.

STEINHEISER, RICK, and JOHN T. GUTHRIE. "Perceptual and Linguistic Processing of Letters and Words by Normal and Disabled Readers," *Journal of Reading Behavior*, 9, 3 (Fall 1977), 217-225.

Investigates three groups of readers—disabled, age-matched normal, and reading-level matched normal—in terms of response latencies on word matching and sentence completion exercises. Results suggest an interconnectedness of perceptual and semantic processing.

WEAVER, WENDELL W. "The Word as the Unit of Language," *Journal of Reading*, 10 (January 1967), 262-268.

Presents a survey of psycholinguistic research and thought on language units, particularly words. Demonstrates that words are neither self-evident nor functionally valid units.